Nationhood Interrupted

Nationhood Interrupted

Revitalizing *nêhiyaw* Legal Systems

Sylvia McAdam (Saysewahum)

PURICH
PUBLISHING
LIMITED
SASKATOON, SK. CANADA

Purich Books, an imprint of UBC Press
2029 West Mall
Vancouver, BC, V6T 1Z2
www.purichbooks.ca

26 25 24 23 22 21 20 19   5 4 3

Printed in Canada on FSC-certified ancient-forest-free paper (100% post-consumer recycled) that is processed chlorine- and acid-free.

Library and Archives Canada Cataloguing in Publication

McAdam, Sylvia, author
    Nationhood interrupted : revitalizing Nêhiyaw legal
Systems / Sylvia McAdam (Saysewahum).

ISBN 978-1-895830-80-4 (pbk.)

    1. Cree Indians – Legal status, laws, etc. – Canada. 2. Cree Indians – Social life and customs. 3. Oral tradition – Canada. I. Title.

KE7749.C88M33 2015   342.7108'72   C2015-900050-5   KF8228.C88N35 2015

Canadä

UBC Press gratefully acknowledges the financial support for our publishing program of the Government of Canada (through the Canada Book Fund), the Canada Council for the Arts, and the British Columbia Arts Council.

Printed and bound in Canada by Friesens

Edited, designed, and typeset by Donald Ward.
Cover design by D.J. Olson, Olson Information Design.
Cover image by Wenona Partridge.

Dedication

THIS BOOK IS DEDICATED to all residential school survivors. The knowledge shared here is your inherent birthright: may it heal, nurture, and guide you. For the ones who died in those horrible schools, you are my heroes.

As well, this is in memory of all the missing and murdered Indigenous women: may your journey to the spirit world be peaceful and swift. May your families find solace and answers until we all join you in the spirit world.

To all the Elders and knowledge keepers who have made their journey to the spirit world, may this book honour your knowledge and wisdom. This book does not profess to provide all of our Indigenous knowledge. It is merely an opening to an ancient and beautiful history and world understanding.

I promised my cousin Marie McAdam during a hospital visit that her name would not be forgotten. She is in the spirit world now. Dear Marie, if you are with me, I hope in this small step I have kept my promise.

To all my deceased relatives, including my siblings Raymond, Rosie, Darryl, and Sterling: you are always in our family's hearts and never far from our memories. To my ex mother-in-law, Yvonne Rose Morin: you have shown me that the journey to the spirit world can be fearless, peaceful, and gentle, as your voice always was.

To my many grandparents and great grandparents whose voices held the memories of our freedom, liberation, and Nationhood: you instilled in me the fortitude to continue protecting our Indigenous sovereignty and self-determination while the colonizers' systems seem hell bent to destroy it. I will honour you by continuing to protect and defend the very things that you have given your lives to preserve.

Contents

Foreword

IT IS THE FIRST SNOWFALL OF SASKATOON as I write this foreword. It is a reminder of the beginning of our seasonal conversation about the sacredness of spiritual teaching. A time for sharing deep knowledge about the sacred and raising deep questions about our relationship to the great mystery that surrounds us. No longer concerned with nourishing the summer plants, the vast spiritual guardians can now turn to the endless questions of the *nêhiyaw* or Cree nation and other Aboriginal people. The intimate relationship over the generations has developed into the accumulated wisdom, insights, experiences, and prophecy of *nêhiyaw* knowledge system and a long and rich legal tradition, which have been taught to the youth in most generations but has been disrupted by Canadian colonialism and Indian residential schools in the last three generations.

Sylvia McAdam has been extraordinarily nourished by *nêhiyaw* language and consciousness as well as understanding of the Canadian legal traditions. The educational process has generated a uniquely blessed comprehension of *nêhiyaw* law, the interrelated spiritual, ecological, and human laws. For more than three decades, Sylvia has been consistently searching to understand the *nêhiyaw* language, knowledge system, and legal tradition. She has used the *nêhiyaw* language and law to frame her legal consciousness. She has animated her legal consciousness and responsibilities to the ecology by generating the powerful and global Idle No More movement, which is described in the book, to awaken Indigenous people to protect the treaties and land.

From her deep understanding of *nêhiyaw* consciousness and Canadian legal traditions, it is unequivocally crucial that she translate and explain the *nêhiyaw* knowledge system and law, rather than have them explained for them or to them by others. *nêhiyaw* consciousness is interwoven with a deeply embedded knowledge, both in an unconscious and conscious manner that have defied the forced assimilation to Eurocentric thought. What is of primary importance is that the *nêhiyaw* recover their own voice about these gifts of their ancestors. The *nêhiyaw* knowledge system and the dynamic of this legal consciousness — too often ignored, too often dominated by Eurocentric simplification, essentialization, and dichotomization — risk misunderstanding by the imported common and civil law systems. Whether *nêhiyaw* or others use the awareness of the importance of the knowledge system and law to change themselves or to maintain their view may be of secondary importance. This awareness will not undermine the resilience of the *nêhiyaw* to maintain and restore their knowledge system and legal traditions.

The question of the law of Aboriginal nations has emerged as the most promising development in Canadian law. The common and civil law has a patchy track record at best, in engaging with Aboriginal legal traditions and systems. Nevertheless, Aboriginal law is the essential foundation and background for understanding Aboriginal and treaty rights affirmed in the Constitution of Canada. The Supreme Court of Canada has affirmed that the law of the Aboriginal peoples survived the assertion of sovereignty by the British monarchy, where retained in the treaties, and survived the jurispathic operation of the common and civil law that deemed them invalid. The continuing role of *sui generis* Aboriginal law is an imperative in the transition to constitutional supremacy, a pluralistic rule of law in Canada, and the constitutional reconciliations.

This book is structured with the teaching traditions of *nêhiyaw*, recreating the deep stories and ceremonies of this performance-based legal tradition. This book reveals an introduction and synthesis of the law of the *nêhiyaw*. This book insightfully and with sensitivity opens up the complexities and beauty of the *nêhiyaw* law. It helps us to comprehend the *nêhiyaw's* powerful and convincing concept of justice. It provides a basis for positive change when engaging with the complexity of nêhiyaw law. It is an invaluable addition to the knowledge base of Aboriginal law for the Canadian legal profession, and any policy maker or advocate. Aboriginal laws are significant for a range of endeavours in justice reform and rule of law to overcome the past denial and avoidance of Aboriginal law, to bring out the inherent complexities of constitutional law, and to providing the basis for the delivery of essential services and economic development.

Sa'ke'j Henderson, IPC, FRSC
Native Law Centre of Canada
November 2014

9

Preface

NÊHIYAWAK WALKED AND LIVED ON THESE LANDS long before the Europeans came here. They lived in vibrant, beautiful, and sustainable societies and nations. There are laws that guided and directed them, original instructions in harmony and reverence with creation. *manitow wiyinikêwina* and *nêhiyaw wiyasiwêwina* are the "laws" often referred to in history as "strong moral codes" or rules. When I sought out permission from my parents, Francis and Juliette McAdam (Saysewahum), recognized knowledgeable Elders of our nation, they clearly stated that only the physical laws could be written down and not the spiritual laws. Which posed a challenge, at best; the physical and spiritual are intimately intertwined, but not impossible to speak about as separately as possible. You will read "glimpses" of spirituality and hints of meanings far more than I could write about.

When seeking knowledge from *nêhiyawak*, a protocol is used. When I sought permission, I approached certain knowledge keepers and Elders with protocol. This protocol is integral and important when retrieving *nêhiyaw* knowledge, teachings, and history. The accepted general protocol is to offer tobacco, a cloth (a broadcloth either one or two metres long), and a gift. The colour of the broadcloth is pre-determined by asking the Elder or knowledge keeper prior to the initial meeting. Be prepared to spend time with the Elder or knowledge keeper. For further suggested information please read "Cultural Teachings: First Nations Protocols and Methodologies." I had to spend hours listening to the teachings and history of my people. Many times I drove my parents to the lands where this history happened. I went to the graves of my people killed by disease and residential schools. Some children refused to go with the Indian agent and priests so they would run away deep into the forests. Many of them would die from hunger or the cold and would be buried where they were found. Other times, it would be the streams or waterways that would be the source of a story and how the people would stop and camp in certain areas. Much patience is required to learn the oral history.

Permission is granted when the protocol is accepted, thus the birth of this book. After much research and listening to my parents sharing their knowledge about *manitow wiyinikêwina* and *nêhiyaw wiyasiwêwina*, it was decided it is time to share something that should have been shared with my people from the time of their birth to their death. An inherent right to know the laws that must guide and direct their every act and actions with their words, thoughts, feelings, and physical movements.

Even as I write each chapter, I smudge continuously. Smudging means to light up sweetgrass or sage, allowing the smoke to fill the air. After it's lit, I would move my hands in a forward cupping motion to bring the smoke toward me as if I were washing my face, ears, and eyes. The smoke clears the mind and prayers are carried to the spirit keepers or to the Creator. This has been done by my people since time immemorial; every action of sharing knowledge must be smudged and prayed about. Before this book goes to print, it will have been taken to one of my people's lodges to be blessed. Then it will be ready for the public to read.

The knowledge shared here has been interrupted by systems of the colonizer; revitalizing this knowledge is critical and integral to Indigenous nationhood — for this book, *nêhiyaw* nationhood.

Acknowledgements

THERE WERE TIMES THAT MY DETERMINED ACTIONS to be free have alienated me from the larger dominant society and sometimes even from the Indigenous Nations. It was during those times that true friendships developed and have continued no matter how much time has passed. I will not forget the years in which Angela Demerais, Lisa Albert, Beverly Albert, Geraldine Albert, and Rema Albert along with Linda and Dennis Netmaker have stood by me, never wavering in their friendship. Thank you for that: I cannot say enough how much your friendship gave me the courage to keep moving forward; to believe some day our people will have freedom. Freedom cannot be only for one, it must be for all.

Instrumental in carrying and sharing the important Indigenous knowledge and teachings collected in this book are my parents, Juliette and Francis McAdam (Saysewahum): they were the "hidden" children when the Indian agent and priests came for the children. I am forever grateful for the knowledge they carry to this day because their parents wanted to preserve our teachings and history through their children by hiding them. I am also grateful they passed on the gift of my people's language to their children. It is the use of language which gave me the foundation to retrieve the laws of my people.

For my children, Autumn Rayne, Storm, Victoria, Richard, Amanda, Jenna, and Angela, thank you for your patience and for understanding when I could not be there for you. There are other young people whom I have come to regard with fondness; they are Tyrese Thundervoice Partridge, Sarah Demerais, Rylan Smallchild, Heather Robinson, and Mike Scott. This book is for the young people. You are the reason this knowledge will carry on: may it guide you for our peoples' future and for our self-determination.

To my siblings, Tony, Kurtis, Dion, Arnold, Corrine, Agnes, and Doris, *kinanâskomitinâwâw mistahi*. Thank you especially to my brother Dion for your courage to live and the will to be with us here in the physical world.

Before Idle No More began, the land called out to me. When I began my journey my ex-sister-in-law, Cynthia Beryl Lachance, patiently and unquestioningly helped post our signs and camped out on the land with me. Her presence during that time gave me the audacity to keep questioning and to keep going. Thank you also to my nephews Kesik and Snow for always being there to walk with me when others were too afraid. May you always remember our lands and waters of *okimâw* Saysewahum's peoples; let this book be your shield.

Through Idle No More, I have gained an international family that I miss to this day; Deepa Naik and Trenton Oldfield with baby Fawn, you are courage and truth — thank you for that. My guide through London, United Kingdom, Brian Soloman — may you keep dancing your resistance wherever your feet may land. To Ron Barnes in Geneva, thank you for manoeuvering me through a difficult place and time; may your beautiful voice continue to carry down the halls of the United Nations. I also want to thank the International Human Rights Association of American Minorities (IHRAAM), especially Diana Kly, Chantal Perrault, and Barrister Majid Tramboo, for being a shining light in a place when I was trying to understand the international discourse. Even as you represented minorities, you supported and assisted Indigenous voices that have been silenced for so long. I cannot say how grateful I am to James Anaya, who was the United Nations Special Rapporteur for Indigenous Issues at the time when we met with him. His efforts gave me strength to keep believing Indigenous peoples will have their humanity and self-determination respected and honoured.

In many ways my mentors and friends have affected the making of this book, whether it be spiritual, or in many discussions and debates. I am grateful to Arlene Seegerts, Sharon Venne, Shannon Houle, Janice Makokis, Tori Cress, Lynda Kitchikeesic Juden, Kamao Cappo, Shannon Avison, Spencer Mann, Anna Popham, Shawn Johnston, Alex Wilson, Erica Lee, Chastity Delorme, Harvey Knight, Dion Tootoosis, Diane Corbin, Niigaan (James) Sinclair, Leah Gazan, Gloria Lee, Russ Diabo, Arthur Manual, Lee Crowchild, Sa'ke'j Youngblood Henderson, Colby Tootoosis,

Mylan Tootoosis, Jimmy O'Chiese and his wife Cynthia Cowan. and all those that I may have forgotten from my many Facebook conversations. For those particular ladies with whom I shared laughter and much-needed time away, thank you Jennifer Cook, Connie Cook, Cathy Merrick, Helga Cheesequay, and Daphne Sinclair for your beautiful laughter and contagious joy for life.

Pictures convey a story, my friend Marcel Petit from m.pet productions donated much of his time and energy to rescan some of the old pictures utilized here — his expertise made it possible to use these images so that I may share them; thank you for that, Marcel. As well, a great big thank you to Arok Wolvengrey and his wife Jean Okimâsis for donating their time and energy to spell *nêhiyaw* words into roman orthography, it has added life to the words.

To my kind and loving spirit sister, Sheelah McLean: I don't believe this journey together is a coincidence. I am proud to walk it with you even during those times when we stumble; our journey is a powerful gift and still continues despite ourselves.

Most of all, I am forever grateful for Idle No More and all the grassroots people who answered our call for help. To the four corners of our beautiful mother earth, thank you; know always that my prayers go out to each and every one of you who shared your stories, your songs, your voices, your art, your drums, and your resistance. We've tasted our collective power and freedom; there is no turning back.

Finally, thank you to Purich Publishing for your patience and in nudging me forward each time I became far too busy. Your belief and support has made this book come alive.

Many, many thanks to our ancestors who suffered and persisted so that I may live, so that all of us and our descendants may live.

May the spirit and intent of Treaty 6 persevere. Let decolonization begin and endure so that my people not only survive but flourish.

Canada Council Conseil des arts
for the Arts du Canada

êkosi

The author acknowledges the support of the Canada Council for the Arts, which last year invested $157 million to bring the arts to Canadians throughout the country.

Nous remercions le Conseil des arts du Canada de son soutien. L'an dernier, le Conseil a investi 157 millions de dollars pour metre de l'art dans la vie des Canadiennes et des Canadiens de tout le pays.

Disclaimer

IN RESPECT OF THE DENE, NAKAWÊ, LAKOTA, DAKOTA, and Nakota, and Cree knowledge keepers and Elders, the information provided in this book is only a general guide to the protocols and methodologies of First Nations. The importance of following appropriate guidance from respected First Nations Elders and knowledge keepers in these matters is paramount. In no way should any reader of this book undertake First Nations protocols and methodologies without appropriate guidance from respected First Nations Elders and knowledge keepers.

There is diversity among the First Nations cultures of Saskatchewan. The protocols and methodologies of these First Nations cultures vary. In particular, it should also be noted that not all First Nations have the same "rites of access," and Elders or other knowledge keepers should be consulted for appropriate protocols.

tawâw niwâhkômâkanak

IT IS THE TASK AND DUTY OF AN OSKÂPÊWS to lead the way for the Nation when they are needed to do so for any event, activity, or ceremony. An *oskâpêws* is a "sacred helper" who understands and knows the *nêhiyaw* laws. It is in keeping with our *nêhiyaw* laws and protocols that this very important book has been created and written. This book is similar to a sharing and teaching ceremony so it is my task to speak to you before you continue on your learning journey.

It is suggested that you say prayers and for those who use "smudge," I suggest you smudge before proceeding to read. Prayers and smudge always must lead the way when a person is seeking and learning knowledge. For each one of you who are about to read this book, what you are doing is seeking knowledge. The knowledge shared here is of a spiritual nature, this is why you must enter this knowledge-seeking with smudge and prayer. When a person seeks knowledge, the knowledge moves, shapes, and changes their thoughts and their spirit. This is especially true for knowledge that is spiritually based. If need be, prayer and smudging throughout this book would be appropriate.

After your prayers are done, read the contents of this book with compassion, respect, and courage. It is written for the generations to come to sustain and nurture the nationhood of the mighty *nêhiyaw* Nation. The *nêhiyaw* people have been here since time immemorial: it is time to share our laws and our teachings. You may now proceed with your learning.

kinanâskomitinâwâw,
Allan Joe (A. J.) Felix
Treaty 6 citizen
Sturgeon Lake First Nation

Nationhood Interrupted

Revitalizing *nêhiyaw* Legal Systems

CHAPTER ONE

Introduction

ahâw ... pîhtokwêk

Aboriginal (Indigenous) Hunters always speak as if the keepers of
the spirits of nature are in control of the hunt. The hunters do not
believe that their awareness or skills have any controlling authority in their hunt. They say the forces of nature are watching them,
know everything on their minds, and what and how they behave
in the hunt. The spiritual forces decide which animals will be made
available and caught, thus determining the success of the hunt. The
creation of this book followed this pattern, with the many spirits
and forces controlling its production and contents.

— Sa'ke'j Henderson[1]

"AHÂW . . . PÎHTOKWÊK" IS AN ANCIENT CALL from the *oskâpêwis* giving
permission for all who are attending the event, ceremony, or activity to
come in. It is the sacred "helpers," male and female, who lead the way for
any *nêhiyaw* gathering, event, or ceremony. So it is for this book. All
that is contained here ideally would have been shared and taught to all
nêhiyaw people, and all who share in their circle. So this spirit of sharing
and transferring informs the knowledge provided for readers. For as long
as the collective memory of the *nêhiyawak* (Crees) can recall, their sacred
ceremonies have existed with the *oskâpêwis* (helper) leading each way. The
term *oskâpêwis* carries profound obligations and responsibilities guided by
nêhiyaw laws, protocols, and methodologies — task and a role not easily
met. Each role, each teaching, each learning is believed to heal and nurture
the soulflame of each human being. When a ceremonial song calls out the
spirit keepers of *nêhiyaw* laws, the vibrations are felt through the genera-

tions: a connection binding all the Creator's children and creations.

The *nêhiyaw kêhtê-ayak* have historically been wary of writing down the laws of their nations. The languages and traditions of the Indigenous peoples are disappearing at a heartbreaking rate,[2] and, with this in mind, the following statement gives concession to begin writing down *nêhiyaw* laws. But the spiritual laws can never be written down:

> They need to be taught both ways in respect. When I hear, "What are we going to do?" as I heard here today, perhaps, we now have to seriously rely on the knowledgeable elders and how things should be properly written on paper. I said that today, certain oral knowledge has to be written on paper. We have to call on our elders, the ones that know how things were conducted and how they observed, listened and properly learned this vital information. We need to go to these things and use them as protection for the future. We have to teach our youth these things.[3]

Each human being has a profound and sacred beginning. This beginning is believed to come from a sacred place where the Creator resides. The Indigenous human birth teaching is shared on the understanding that, when we are born into our humanity, we are born into our nation's obligations and responsibilities. The first human being's arrival was prepared when the Creator gathered together all manner of animals from all over the world. After the earth preparations were done, the Creator prepared in the spirit world.

In the spirit world, a flame was prepared: this flame would be called *ahcahk iskotêw*, the soulflame. The soulflame is a gift from the Creator and with it comes *pimâtisiwin* (life). This life carries many obligations and responsibilities. Prior to the arrival of the Europeans, a *nêhiyaw* child would have been taken into a ceremony, a form of welcoming him/her into the nation. This ceremony is performed for every child with prayer and with *wâhkôhtowin* (kinship). *wâhkôhtowin* is constantly affirmed and enforced throughout the child's life. Since European contact, the Indigenous birth has been disrupted, and much of the teachings that are involved were illegalized through the *Indian Act*, along with the ceremonies.

The ancient echoes of *nêhiyaw* laws can still be heard in the languages, lands, and cultures of the Treaty 6 *nêhiyawak*. When the Europeans arrived in Canada, Indigenous nations lived in diverse, vibrant, and structured societies. It is likely that all the Indigenous nations had their own laws and legal systems which guided and directed the people in their daily interactions with families, communities, and other nations. Treaty 6 is created on the foundations of the *nêhiyaw* laws and legal systems from the understanding of the *nêhiyaw* people.

Everything in creation has laws and these are called *manitow wiyinikêwina*. The human laws are called *nêhiyaw wiyasiwêwina*. The Indigenous people are not a lawless people; the Creator's laws are strict and inform every part of a person's life. It is these laws that governed and guided in the days when Europeans did not walk the territories of Indigenous people. These laws still exist and can be revitalized.

nêhiyaw laws are in the songs, the ceremonies, and in all the sacred sites. The land is intertwined in a most profound manner, so to separate the two would mean death to many aspects of *nêhiyaw* culture. All the laws combined with creations are called *manitow wiyinikêwina*, meaning Creator's laws; however, for the human laws, they are called *nêhiyaw wiyasiwêwina*.

COURTESY SYLVIA MCADAM

My grandparents. His name is Frizzly Bear and his uncle was Big Bear. Her name is ka-kwêskapîstawat.

At the time of treaty making in Treaty 6 territory, these laws guided the process. When treaties became binding, it became a ceremonial covenant of adoption between two families. "kiciwâminawak, our cousins: that is what my elders said to call you."[4] In nêhiyaw law, the treaties were adoptions of one nation by another. At Treaty 6 the nêhiyawak adopted the Queen and her children. We became relatives.[5] When your ancestors came to this territory, kiciwâminawak, our law applied.[6] These kinship relationships were active choices, a state of relatedness or connection by adoption.[7] Indigenous laws, specifically nêhiyaw (Cree) laws, were the vehicle that drove the process and the signing. Many of these laws have not been recorded or understood; however, they are imperative in treaty understanding and negotiations. It is these same laws that became hidden through the processes of colonialism and must now be revitalized for the wellbeing of the nêhiyaw Nation.

The women's teachings are the educational system of the *nêhiyaw* Nation. There existed a group of women called *okihcitâwiskwêwak* whose role was to provide the legal "system" of the *nêhiyaw* people. These women invoked the laws and provided remedies on a case-by-case basis, depending on the situation or circumstances before them. As well, the women are the first to carry each child born into the nation.

Children are expected to assist in braiding hair, but most importantly, our mother earth's hair. Mother earth's hair is the sweetgrass (*wîhkaskwa*). Sweetgrass is integral and essential in any *nêhiyaw* ceremony; it is difficult to conduct a ceremony without this sacred item. The picking and braiding of sweetgrass is a ceremony in itself, and requires knowledge and patience on the part of the picker. Our mother earth's teachings and the women's teachings cannot be told without one or the other because they are interconnected.

The gift of language, *kinêhiyawêwininaw*, is a powerful and sacred gift a parent can give a child. This same gift has been given to the human beings by the Creator. The *nêhiyawak* have been given this language, which is heard all across much of Treaty 6 territory. The *nêhiyawak* are the dominant nation for most of Alberta, Saskatchewan, and Manitoba. The language is complex and embodies terms that are difficult to translate into English; some words have no English equivalent. When *nêhiyawak* enter into their ceremonial lodges, a spiritual language is spoken, words are shared which are not heard in the "everyday" language. The language provides the names of sacred sites, lakes, rivers, and many other important land areas. Language is believed to have a sacred spirit, and this spirit will leave if the language is not utilized. There is a spirituality embedded in the words, songs, prayers, and history. Oral tradition depends on language to transfer and transmit the critical and integral terms, names, histories, and songs of Indigenous peoples. The English language is adequate but the Indigenous language is preferable.

pimâcihowin is *nêhiyaw isîhcikêwin* (culture/way of doing things) and is profoundly connected to *kikâwînaw askiy* (mother earth). This speaks to a pre-existing livelihood: hunting, gathering, and fishing; a form of Indigenous agriculture pre-existed through knowledge of the land. However, with the advent of the numbered treaties, *pimâcihowin* included agriculture as a "new" way of life. This is not to diminish the importance of land before the numbered Treaties, for without the land and its resources no ceremonies could be done nor could people live. The songs, ceremonies, and culture carry the history and knowledge of *nêhiyawak* for all time. The hunters' songs are interconnected with the lands and waters, even to the creatures that live deep in the earth.

Nationhood is primarily about land, language, and culture. Gaining an awareness of Indigenous laws will provide non-Indigenous people insight into the thoughts, worldview, and nationhood of Indigenous people before and during the numbered Treaty-making process. The cultures of Indigenous peoples are diverse and unique. In this, *iyiniw miyikowisiwin* are the First Nations laws, First Nations understandings of Creation and sacred relationships with all of Creation.[8] The Indigenous people's elements of Nationhood are tied to sovereignty; "when these factors no longer exist then we become assimilated into the dominant culture therefore face the possibility of losing the uniqueness and sovereignty of First Nations."[9]

nêhiyaw history is not written in the history books of *môniyâwak*; the beautiful and powerful *nêhiyaw* history is written in the lands and waters. It's in the pictographs, petroglyphs, rock markings, in the ghost dance bundles, sacred sites, and the final resting places of Indigenous peoples. *nêhiyaw* history is believed to be "written" in the blood memory and in the spiritual memories of its peoples.

This book cannot stress enough the importance of maintaining the nationhood of Indigenous peoples. Even as Indigenous peoples "borrow" terms to apply to their situation, it no way diminishes or negates their standing among any nation in the world. This book is written in the hope and dream of revitalizing *nêhiyaw* laws within the *nêhiyaw* Nation, so they will raise lawful Indigenous citizens for their respective nation. This creates a majority of individuals who will become lawful and responsible citizens, thereby revitalizing the inherent rights and structures of Indigenous peoples. This is the ideal.

PHOTO COURTESY THE AUTHOR

These are my maternal grandparents, Thomas Whitefish and his wife, Mary Whitefish (née Thomas). My grandfather was a hereditary headman until he passed away; my grandmother was nakawê *and part of Big Bear's people.*

CHAPTER TWO

Soulflame

Our human birth — our Indigenous birth, the Creator gave this
to us and Spirit of the tree to bless us with. It was at that time the
Creator blessed us before our human birth, from the Creator's flame,
a "soulflame" — the soulflame is there to look after our bodies, our
minds and our souls. We picked from the Creator's flame before our
human birth — the tiny flame we picked became our soul, which is
called a soulflame that is half man half woman and when we go to
pick our soulflame — it is then that it's decided whether you would
be male or female or what you would look like.

— Barry Ahenakew[1]

Soulflame: Understanding the Gift of *nêhiyaw pimâtisiwin* (life)

Everything has a beginning, so it is for *pimâtisiwin. nêhiyawak* understand
pimâtisiwin as a gift from the Creator. This gift of *pimâtisiwin* is to follow
the strict truths that a person seeks; once the knowledge is shared, there are
formal and respectful submissions of gratitude.[2] To be born *nêhiyaw* is to
be born into the lands, cultures, and languages of the people as well as the
responsibilities and obligations.

The Indigenous *nêhiyaw* birth of each citizen has been disrupted. In fact,
there are multiple disruptions, causing nations of Indigenous people to
lose their connection to the laws that the Creator has given them to live by.
These disruptions are the genocide and colonization of the *nêhiyaw* people
in Treaty 6 territory.

Many outstanding authors have written about the impacts of genocide
and colonialism, and their continued effects on a Nation of Indigenous

people in what is now called Canada. Many communities are experiencing epidemic proportions of violence and suicide.[3] Family violence is in a crisis state[4] for many Indigenous communities. These are all facts and will not be discussed in detail in this book, given all the resources available for persons to inform themselves. Needless to say, it is the impacts of genocide and colonialism that have disrupted the sacred birth of the *nêhiyaw* people.

When a nation does not understand their laws or live by them, it creates a void, a state of lawlessness. This lawless state has created an imbalance that has spanned several generations. This is not to say it is irreparable: this lawless state is reparable, but the transference and transmission of *nêhiyaw* laws have been disrupted, along with other aspects of *nêhiyaw* life.

This is especially true when exploring effects on the role of *nêhiyaw* women; this is not to minimize the impacts on men. The law keepers are the *nêhiyaw* women,[5] but with the advent of the *Indian Act*, the status of women and the illegalizing of *nêhiyaw* ceremonies had a terrible consequence on parenting and the transferring of Indigenous knowledge. It is this knowledge that is crucial and critical in creating a foundation of laws in which each child is nurtured and raised. Each *nêhiyaw* ideally should have been raised with these teachings and knowledge from cradle to death; it is their inherent knowledge.

The teaching is about the spiritual journey before human birth; it begins in that spiritual realm in which the Creator, the life giver, resides. When it is time for human beings to be born, they make their way to a flame. This flame is similar in shape and form to the sun: it is called *manitow iskotêw*[6] (Creator's flame). The culture, language, and lands of the *nêhiyawak* (Crees) play a critical role in the lives of *nêhiyaw* children. *nêhiyaw* children are not born "Canadian"; rather, they are born into their nation with a distinct "bundle" of inherent rights and Treaty rights.

In the spiritual realm of the Creator, the potential human makes his or her journey to the *manitow iskotêw*; they pick a tiny flame from it and place this flame at the top of their head — the "soft spot."[7] It is believed this soft spot carries the soulflame which has been referred to as the soul or spirit. It is then a person makes their way to the earth and is born into their nation's obligations, responsibilities, and gifts. Many times *nêhiyaw* Elders during prayers or ceremony declare "all my relations" — this reference is not limited to their nation, but rather to all nations of the world because it is believed we come from the same flame, thus making us relatives.

A *nêhiyaw* child is born with many gifts; *nêhiyawêwin* (language), *pimâtisiwin* (life), *pimâcihowin* (livelihood). More specifically, there are four gifts given to them: emotional, mental, physical, and spiritual. All four have to be in balance with each other, utilizing the *nêhiyaw* laws as the foundation at all times. These gifts have been described in a diagram called the medicine wheel. The medicine wheel symbolizes these gifts, while its four directions represent balance. There are various versions and uses of the medicine wheel by different tribes,[8] but all of them are divided into four distinct realms which can indicate the four grandfathers, the four winds, the four cardinal directions, and many other significant sets of four.[9]

However, for this chapter it is applied to the four gifts mentioned. The four gifts are nurtured by the laws, especially the law of *miyo-ohpikinâwasowin*. Further, one of the most important laws that speak to raising a *nêhiyaw* child is *miyo-ohpikinâwasowin* or *ohpikinâwasowin*.[10] *miyo-* means good, *ohpikinâwasowin* means child-rearing or raising. *miyo-ohpikinâwasowin* directs parents to raise their children to become lawful *nêhiyaw* citizens for their respective *nêhiyaw* nations. This law is taught to all citizens of the *nêhiyaw* nations from cradle to death; their responsibilities do not end when their child reaches a certain age. It is a lifelong responsibility.

The physical gift is the body. The body requires food, water, and whatever a body needs for a healthy life. The physical body's health is reflected by one's access to healthy food, healthy water, physical activity, and so on. How a person treats their body and their access to things that would contribute to a healthy body nurtures and sustains the physical gift. This same access to healthy and nurturing ingredients apply to the other three gifts.

The emotional gift is nurtured and sustained by healthy kinships and relationships. However, the environment plays a critical role in contributing to the healthy surroundings to raise a child. The emotional gift is not limited to the physical, but is nurtured by the spiritual as well. This spiritual emotional nurturing is done through the spiritual keepers who protect and guide the child until death. The emotional gift is nurtured by love, respect, kindness, compassion, and so forth.

The mental gift is nurtured by language, culture, teachings, laws, and Indigenous knowledge, but is not limited to this. This is the intelligence and thinking given to humans. This gift is affected by access to education (Indigenous or otherwise), access to Indigenous knowledge, access to the gift of language, and world view. As a child grows, their mental aspect is fed by their environment, family, and sense of identity. Everything that impacts and contributes to their mental health is absorbed through this thinking gift.

The spiritual gift is that part of *nêhiyawak* in which spirituality connects them to the Creator, to the life-giver. The connection is what sustains and nurtures the spiritual gift, the ability to *ka-manitowîmot*, meaning to call out to the Creator. Its various teachings about land, spirituality, laws, and kinship sustain and nurture a child to encourage prayer with the gifts given to them. The gift of prayer, recognizing each teaching connects humans to creation by the understanding we all have a spirit. The spiritual connects the unseen to a more human level through songs, ceremonies, land, animals; all of creation.

When all four of these gifts are limited or withheld, then the child is not nurtured to their fullest potential. However, these limitations can be corrected later in life so that the adult can reconnect with the Creator and find their way back into a balanced state. When a person is in a balanced state they utilize all four of their gifts as a way to honour the Creator by following the laws and ways in which they are given to live. In other words, their life honours the Creator and all laws.

The journey of each *nêhiyaw* person begins in the spiritual world with the Creator, the life giver. Human birth is sacred and profound because of the gift of the soulflame. The reference that a child is a gift is that much more understood: "a newly born baby is the closest a human being will ever get to the Creator."[11]

"Welcoming into Our Nation" Ceremony

Ceremonial songs invoke the ancient vibrations of the rattles and drums opening the way into another realm. The life giver gifted the *nêhiyawak* many teachings and ways to access the spiritual realm that inform and guide the people. It is this connection that stirs the hearts of a circle of women enveloped in the smoke of sweetgrass waiting for the arrival of a new citizen to be brought into their lodge. The sweet grass smoke is strong as it swirls and surrounds the interior. The preparations involved all the women from *kâ-omîkwanisicik iskwêwak* to *okihcitâwiskwêwak*. Each role is critical and integral, and is as ancient as the people in which it serves.

The following is an account from an Elder woman raised in the traditions of the *nakawê* and *nêhiyaw* people. Juliette McAdam (Saysewahum) was raised with her *nakawê* grandmother who spoke in earnest about the teachings of women and childbirth. Her grandmother's name was *kiskâwapiwisk* (sits with the morning sun).

What makes this account unique is that Juliette (the speaker), Juliette's mother Mary, and Juliette's maternal grandmother did not attend an Indian residential school, so the information and knowledge is relatively intact. This was the era when the Indian residential schools had a policy to assimilate In-

COURTESY SYLVIA MCADAM

This is kîsikâwapiwisk *(sits with the morning sun), the last of the* okicitaw iskwewak *of her region. She was also the last woman to carry memories of the* okicitaw iskwewak *(law keepers) conducting a woman's ceremony before the making of Treaty 6. She is my great grandmother, my maternal grandfather's mother.*

digenous children. The history of Juliette McAdam's family involved family members that "hid" away their children in the hunting lands. It was during these times of hiding that the women spoke to her and insisted that she keep the voices of the women alive. It is these accounts that inform this chapter.

Mrs. McAdam (Saysewahum) recalls lengthy conversations with her grandmother recounting the lodges of the women. There are songs to comfort women during childbirth and many other songs to assist in the *miyo-ohpikinâwasowin* law. These songs are sung in the lodges of women,[12] each song is different in its purpose. Some of the songs are for welcoming a child into the physical world and are sung in the *okihcitâwiskwêwikamik* (clan mother/warrior woman lodge). The following statement describes the lodge of women as they welcome a newly born baby into their community and into their nation:

"*niya ôma kohkom*" (I am your grandmother) were the first words said to a child held by the Eldest woman amongst select women sitting in a ceremonial circle to welcome a new citizen for the *nêhiyaw* Nation. The intonation is almost in a revered voice, for the women understand as they carry this baby "a newly born baby is the closest a human being will ever get to the Creator." It is with the soulflame and Indigenous birth teaching in their minds as each woman "introduces" herself to the baby. The *nêhiyaw* kinship structure is complex and has terms which determine the place of each relative. It is these terms that each female relative recites followed by such statements as "*niya oma kohkom*" which means "I am your grandmother." This is generally followed with using the kinship term that the baby will know them by for rest of his/her life. Possible the conversation will be saying "I am your mother's mother and you are born for the *nêhiyaw* Nation." The baby is spoken to similar to an adult as they hear the language and the words of *wâhkôhtowin* (kinship) terms. The soulflame is at its brightest and still spiritually connected to the *manitow iskotêw.*[13]

The lodge itself is a *mîkiwâhp* (tipi) and is prepared by the women for this particular "Welcoming into the Nation" ceremony. All the men, with the exception of the father, are not allowed to carry the baby until the *ocisîs* (belly button) has fallen off, then another ceremony called the naming ceremony is conducted.

Typically, the lodge itself is made of tipi poles; the poles are from pine trees taken from the forest. Historically, buffalo hides would have been used to cover the lodge and rocks to hold down the hides. With the disappearance of the buffalo, tipis are now made of canvas. Women own the tipis, so the design of any lodge must be approved by women.[14] A fire would have been burning in the middle with sweetgrass smoke constantly in the air.[15] The circle of the lodge would have seen women leaning on "back rests" of willow rods;[16] there would have been plenty of soft buffalo hide on the ground for sitting.

The preparations include swaddling the baby in a mossbag[17] made of hide; it was the midwives who prepared the baby. After a child is born into their human birth, the parents understand and are guided by many laws on how to raise their child. One of these laws for the *nêhîyawak* is *miyo-ohpikinâwasowin*. *miyo-ohpikinâwasowin* is considered a law on how to "raise children in a good way." This entails preparation for a child's impending birth to preparing a lodge to welcome the child into the nation and readying the *wâspison* (mossbag) to clothing.

The *wâspison* has also been referred to as a cradleboard. The *wâspison* or cradleboard is similar to a carrying bundle designed for babies to be carried in comfort. Babies are wrapped and secured in a *waspison* to create contented sleeps so they won't wake themselves up by uncontrolled movements of their limbs. Further, the *waspison* keeps the baby's backbone and legs straight so that it strengthens neck muscles; it also provides an opportunity for children to enhance their hearing, seeing, and listening while being stimulated by their environment with family and relatives.

The *waspison* is made with love and care; each stitch an expression of affection by the relative making the *wâspison*. The *wâspison* is smudged and blessed because it is to be the *pêpîsis* home for a better part of a year. Most children are not allowed to touch the ground until another ceremony is performed. The use of a hide string is used to secure *pêpîsis* into their *wâspison*: the string is symbolic of the umbilical cord. The string secures *pêpîsis*; just as the umbilical cord gave it life and security, so does this string.

Midwifery is a highly specialized profession;[18] not only are the women gifted in childbirth skills, but they must also have knowledge of the age-old medicines used by our grandmothers and highly prized today.[19] It is these women who are part of the *okihcitâwiskwêwak*; they are a sacred and profound part of the nationhood of the people.

The role of women has been decimated through colonialism and genocide. The term Indian is used to identify Indigenous peoples in Canada through the *Indian Act*. This term is a legal term and is government controlled to access Aboriginal and treaty rights. This system of delineating rights controls and undermines *nêhiyaw* women's authority and jurisdiction over the citizenship of their people. Registration under the *Indian Act* is complex, with many confusing and illogical rules that give preference to Indian men.[20] The unfortunate result is discrimination against women and their descendants as well as undermining the jurisdiction for *nêhiyaw* nations to determine who their citizens are.

The birth of each *nêhiyaw* child is not that of a "Canadian" citizen but rather a citizen of the *nêhiyaw* Nation. Dr. Taiaiake Alfred from the University of Victoria takes this a step further and declares:

We are not Canadians. And why should we be so eager and willing to be citizens of their country? Has the citizenship legally forced on our people a generation ago helped get land back, gain compensation for past injustices, or made our communities healthier? Of course it hasn't (we should also remember that citizenship was rejected by the Elders in most communities). Forty years of citizenship and we're more assimilated now than ever before, and we're losing our languages and traditions at a heartbreaking rate. What citizenship has done over the years is undermine in people's minds the idea that we have a separate existence and distinct collective rights (witness the recent attacks on Mi'kmaq treaty rights — the ignorant Prime Minister saying the "law must be upheld the same for all Canadians" — and the ongoing general effort to force taxes and provincial authority on us, for example). No matter what our lawyers argue or what the judges say about "Aboriginal rights," the tide of public opinion is against us and it's easy to see why the government feels comfortable defying its own Constitution to support the non-Native majority's interest.[21]

PHOTO COURTESY THE AUTHOR

These are the graves of okimâw *(Chief) Saysewahum's (sâh-sêwêham) peoples; I am descended from them. There are hundreds of graves located in Stony Lake. Many of the people died from disease-infested blankets, some from running away from the Indian Agent and priests who came for the children. Some, like my great grandfather Peter Saysewahum, died of natural causes and are buried here.*

Some may consider this a bold statement; however, it is a widely held sentiment and understanding of treaty descendants. This will be affirmed and explained in the following chapters.

Each *nêhiyaw* child has a birth right that is steeped in the history of the land and their kinship with all of creation. They are born into responsibilities and obligations that will guide them from cradle to death. The world of the colonizer is an arm, an apparatus of the colonial state, laws, and policies. To continue applying this apparatus is to continue the assimilation and genocide of Indigenous children, families, and nations. In the spirit and intent of Indigenous sovereignty and treaty, and honouring Indigenous relationships, non-Indigenous people must begin supporting and encouraging Indigenous laws and teachings, in every aspect, and by whatever means possible. How this might look is up to the Indigenous nations working alongside these systems to intervene in colonial narratives, laws, and policies, and collectively work toward dismantling destructive and oppressive systems which have been imposed on Indigenous peoples through colonization. To begin decolonizing systems of the colonizer will inevitably lead to a path of Indigenous self-determination, liberation, and freedom. To do anything less is to allow the genocide to continue.

manitow wiyinikêwina

wîsahkêcâhk[1] went to *okimâwaskwaciy* (Chief Bear Hill in the
Cypress Hills area — *minâtahkâwa*), at the top of *okimâwaskwaciy*,
he sang four songs. As he sang the four songs to the four directions,
the Creator gave him the laws to bring to the people to follow for all
time.

— as told by Francis McAdam (Saysewahum)
Translated by Sylvia McAdam (Saysewahum) and Barry Ahenakew

manitow wiyinikêwina: Rebuilding a Connection

A LOW HUM COULD BE HEARD through the universe, rhythmically broken
by a consistent lull then the hum would repeat itself over and over again.
No human memory could say when this hum began; only in the oral tradition of the *nêhiyaw* and *nakawê* people has it been told through the generations that it is foundational in the creation of mother earth. It is said when
the Creator made *kikâwînaw askiy* (mother earth), the Creator took this
same humming sound from the universe to create the heartbeat of mother
earth.[2] It is this life beat which is heard in the songs of each ceremony
through the beat of *nêhiyaw* drums. Each beat speaks from the spiritual
realm in a sacred manner.

After the earth was created, then the animals were created; the animals were given an *ahcahk[3]* (spirit/soul). It is for this reason that animals have laws they must follow, but no human knows or understands
these laws. Animals, plants, earth, the environment, and all other creations have laws that are interrelated with human laws. When the Creator was planning to create human beings, the Creator called all the

animals together and told them of this plan:

> It is said that when the human being was to be brought to earth, the
> Creator called all the animals of the earth together to ask of them
> certain questions. The animals did gather and were honoured to be
> asked, and the Creator told them about the impending arrival of the
> human being. The animals were excited. The Creator told them that
> the human being would not be like them but would have certain
> gifts. The animals were told to keep the human close to them and
> to help the human when needed. The Creator bestowed upon the
> human being the gift of the knowledge of truth and justice. The only
> way they can find these gifts are if they look inside their hearts, only
> the bravest and purest of heart would be able to do so.[4]

manitow wiyinikêwina means Creator's laws.[5] *manitow* means Creator,
wiyinikêwina means an act similar to a type of weaving. The weaving describes all of creation as bound together, having been given laws. These
laws are interrelated and numerous; no one presumes to know them all;
we are all forever students, with elders being senior students.[6] *manitow
wiyinikêwina* are said to have four parts: human laws, earth laws, spiritual
laws, and animal laws (plants and water are included).[7] These will be discussed in more detail in the next chapter. The physical and spiritual laws
are constantly interrelated and are difficult to separate. Even to speak of
nêhiyaw laws, as well as in the process of writing this information down,
requires some form of prayer. Everything is presumed to have been created
from the realm of the Creator; certainly the human beings who have been
given a soulflame require the utmost respect and prayer.

When *wîsahkêcâhk* went to *okimâwaskwaciy* (Chief Bear Hill in the
Cypress Hills area — *minâtahkâwa*) and the Creator gave him directions, he was told to bring the laws to the people, but specifically it was
the women who became the law keepers. These women would later be
called *okihcitâwiskwêwak*, meaning clan mothers or warrior women.[8]
okimâwaskwaciy means Chief Bear Hill; this area is now called the Cypress Hills. The *okimâwaskwaciy* was once a vibrant, sacred gathering place
for the Indigenous nations. It is now the home of a healing lodge on the
Neekaneet First Nation.

The *nêhiyawak* are guided and directed by the *manitow wiyinikêwina* in their daily activities, events, and ceremonies. The physical human laws will be discussed in this book. The spiritual laws cannot be discussed or revealed: these are the unwritten laws of the people. The physical laws speak to matters of stealing, adultery, murder, proper child rearing, sexual offences, hunting laws, environmental laws, and other such matters of human actions.

The verbal laws of *pâstâmowin* and *ohcinêmowin* address the use of language against human beings (*pâstâmowin*) as well as to creation (*ohcinêmowin*); matters such as gossiping, uttering threats, using profanity against animals or creation. There are laws that speak to every area of a person's life.

KURTIS MCADAM

Janice Makokis and the author on my father's people's lands in the winter of 2013. The panda hat I am wearing was a statement while we walked on the land, for Prime Minister Stephen Harper refused to meet the Nishiyuu walkers when they arrived in Ottawa but instead went to meet the arrival of the pandas, so many people wore panda hats, thinking that if maybe we were pandas he would come to meet us.

It is also important to state that silence and non-action do not exempt any human being from breaking the laws. It's considered a *pâstâmowin* to remain silent or to take no action while a harm is being done to another human being or to anything in creation. In common law, it is called acquiescence; acquiescence is compliance, or when you are silent it is considered consent from a reasonable person. In other words, if a person is getting assaulted and you do nothing to stop or assist, then you have committed a *pâstâmowin* because you failed to prevent or protect another human being. This same idea applies to sharing and speaking to others about knowledge or other such matters; if you do not speak to your children about the laws then you are likely breaking *pâstâmowin*. This applies in cases where people have this knowledge but do not share it or speak of it.

Most important in all of these laws is to remember that they are sacred and are a gift from the Creator. Indigenous peoples are not a lawless people. The *nêhiyawak* have diverse and multi-dimensional laws that are both physical and spiritual. It is believed no human has enough knowledge to write down the spiritual laws; that belongs to the keepers of this knowledge, and they are not human.

All the laws have a spiritual connection; each ceremony is a renewal and reaffirmation to follow them for all time. Even when the human being corrects the laws through the remedies provided, they are reminded that the laws need to be corrected through their relationship with the Creator. It is that relationship that will sustain and nurture them through all trials and tribulations.

a. *nêhiyaw wiyasiwêwina*: Let us speak about *nêhiyaw* laws

So long as men have no respect for the land, they will have no respect for women.

— Francis McAdam (Saysewahum)

"We are not a lawless people"[9] was a statement that echoed through the tiny house of Francis McAdam (Saysewahum) as he sat back on a chair in his kitchen. This statement is shared by many *nêhiyaw* elders and knowledge keepers throughout Treaty 6 territory. When the Europeans arrived on the lands of Indigenous peoples, Indigenous people lived in structured and vibrant nations. Treaty 6 is created on the foundations of the *nêhiyaw* laws and legal systems from the understanding of the *nêhiyaw* people. When treaties became binding, it became a ceremonial covenant of adoption between two families. *kiciwâminawak*, our cousins: that is what my elders said to call you.[10] In *nêhiyaw* law, the treaties were adoptions of one nation by another. During the Treaty 6 making process, the *nêhiyawak* understood it was adoption of the Queen and her descendants, binding the two nations together for all time. We became relatives.[11] When your ancestors came to this territory, *kiciwâminawak*, our law applied.[12] These kinship relationships were active choices, a state of relatedness or connection by adoption.[13] Much of the *nêhiyaw* laws have not been recorded nor understood; however, they are imperative in the treaty understanding, negotiations, and interpretations.

There are people who are the knowledge keepers and have been trained to carry the knowledge and must share when asked, following proper protocol. These knowledge keepers retain their knowledge by oral tradition and knowledge of the land. Oral evidence has been and is still practised by Aboriginal tribes in Canada as a means of recording events.[14] These recorded events are "passed from generation to generation and they have been validated to each generation in the chain; the result is that oral histories are 'enclothe[d] ... with a cloak of trustworthiness.'"[15] The generational chain is maintained by individuals who have been taught since birth to remain diligent and accurate about events significant to the nation. The value of these recordings in oral history are told and retold in ceremonies, in gatherings, and in each household.

Before any event, ceremony, or prayer, protocol must be observed and strictly adhered to. Protocol is the offering of tobacco and various gifts. Tobacco is representative of the pipe; tobacco is sent with every invitation or important message.[16] The following statement conveys the understanding of protocol:

> The Elders' comments allude to formal and long established ways, procedures, and processes that First Nations persons are required to follow when seeking particular kinds of knowledge that are rooted in spiritual traditions and laws. The rules that are applied to this way

of learning are strict, and the seekers of knowledge are required to follow meticulous procedures and processes as they prepare for and enter the "quest for knowledge journey."[17]

The *nêhiyaw* generally follows a particular protocol: the general protocol and methodology is to present the knowledge keeper or elder with tobacco and a cloth (also referred to as print). "The cloth is usually broad cloth and one to two meters [or yards] long. The colour of the print depends on the circumstances."[18] When tobacco and gifts are offered and accepted, this signifies acceptance of the invitation or assent to the proposition stated in the message.[19] Gifts usually accompany the tobacco and cloth and can vary from guns to clothing[20] or money.[21]

The making of this book involved following and providing *nêhiyaw* protocol to knowledge keepers and Elders who shared their teachings and knowledge. It must be noted that protocols and methodologies vary among Indigenous nations. Knowledge keepers are generally described as persons, male and female, who have been raised and taught by knowledgeable Elders and other knowledge keepers who have groomed this individual to carry Indigenous knowledge, teachings, and songs; some will even be ceremonial lodge holders.

When a person seeks knowledge, most *nêhiyaw* elders suggest there is a process in place. The following statement describes this process; however, it is advised that the knowledge seeker speak to the elder for details:

> Seeking knowledge about our ways requires we approach those things in a clean way. In our ways, cleanliness of the mind and body could be achieved only by the selection of a clean place away from human habitation where sweat lodges, ceremonies, fasts, and quiet meditation could be carried out.[22]

The knowledge seeker must abstain from the use of drugs, alcohol, and various other hallucinogenic substances for at least four days prior to meeting with an elder or knowledge keeper.[23] After these processes are followed, the way is paved for the knowledge to be shared. Protocol is always followed, even when speaking about *nêhiyaw* laws.

There are two laws that describe the "act of breaking" a law or laws, but there are subcategories identified from these two main laws. The first one is called *pâstâhowin*, meaning "the breaking of a law(s) against another human being."[24] *pâstâhowin* has also been described as going against natural law:[25] you will suffer retribution for an action against creation.[26] However, this is not quite an accurate description of *pâstâhowin*; it says creation, but *pâstâhowin* applies only when a human breaks a law physically against another human being, not against creation per se. Breaking these laws can bring about divine retribution with grave consequences.[27]

The core of *pâstâhowin* is the root *pâst-*, meaning to "go beyond or over" as in *ê-pâstohtêt*, which translates as "stepping over" something. The verb *pâstâhw-* indicates that one transgresses against another, while a more generic verb, *pâstâho-*, indicates a transgression, and this verb is nominalized by the ending *-win*; hence, *pâstâhowin*, "transgression." Imagine yourself surrounded by lines of laws all your life; there is a line for stealing, murder, etc.; these lines must not be stepped over.[28] When you step over those lines, then you have broken a law and that law needs to be identified.[29] *pâstâhowin* and *ohcinêwin* can apply to any circumstance where the law is not followed, either by action or omission.[30]

pâstâhowin could be the physical breaking of a law(s) through human actions, or it could be applied to the spiritual breaking of laws; however, the spiritual laws cannot be discussed. Spiritual laws are unwritten and must remain in the spiritual realm.

There is a subcategory to *pâstâhowin* which is called *pâstâmowin*. *pâstâmowin* "refers to what someone said which led to something undesirable happening,"[31] or is blasphemous or dangerous speech thought to bring misfortune to the speaker.[32] This law is broken when the person utters threats, gossip, or profanity. It also applies when a person is boastful of his or her success[33] through hunting or other areas of life:

the instance of *pâstâmowin* I remember most vividly occurred when a woman, during the course of a violent argument, uttered the wish that a fatal accident would befall her boyfriend while he was on his trapline. Her mother and sister immediately remonstrated with her for saying such a thing. After her friends departure for the bush, she became frantic with anxiety, repeatedly claiming she would kill herself if her wish came true.[34]

pâstâmowin is about language and its profane use contrary to *nêhiyaw* laws. It's about efficacy, because words have power outside an individual. Once you utter ill wishes, as shown in the above story, the words are outside of you and have a life of their own. Language is a gift from the Creator; therefore, when a person gossips, uses profanity, or utters threats, they are misusing this gift.

The Rock Cree use the related noun *pâstâmowin* to refer to misfortune provoked specifically by speech: *pâstâmow* (verb), "someone brings misfortune on himself by speech."[35] In events such as this, it is not always clear whether *ahcahk* beings are the mediating agents or whether the words themselves are felt to acquire a transitive force that compels their external realization.[36] The spiritual, moral, ethical, and human laws are interrelated. The human activities, omissions, inappropriate communications, and many other acts or inactions are subject to the *nêhiyaw* laws, which are many and vary upon review and discussion.

The second law is called *ohcinêwin*, meaning "the breaking of a law(s) against anything other than a human being."[37] *ohcinêwin* is part of the concept of *pâstâhowin*, and means to suffer in retribution for an action against creation.[38] This law is applied when animals are tortured, land is being polluted, there is an over-harvesting of resources, or *nêhiyaw* hunting laws are broken — in other words, the physical activities of human beings that have a negative impact on their environment. Animals are regarded as persons in their own right; the relationship between the Cree and animal-persons is governed by the same legal considerations that govern human relationships.[39]

"Kill them quickly! You can't let them suffer! Kill 'em quick! You got to give them the same respect you give yourself. That's why a lot of these young trappers don't kill hardly nothing."[40] *ohcinêwin* dictates and directs hunters and others not to cause pain or suffering to animals. Humans can cause pain to animals through certain exploitative techniques, and they have the obligation to minimize this suffering.[41] Many *nêhiyaw* hunters understand and follow this law. However, there are times when animals do suffer and hunters worry that consequences will befall them because of *ohcinêwin*.

Wasteful hunters are called *mîtawâkîw pisiskiwa* — "he plays with an ani-

PHOTO COURTESY THE AUTHOR

This is my son Storm McAdam, taken in 2013 when we joined the Sacred Walkers Journey in Prince Albert. Storm wanted to make a humorous statement in a serious situation by carrying a small sign bearing this message.

mal/animals."⁴² "The verb *wîsakîhîw* refers to acts of wasting animal meat and other products; it refers also to wasting other kinds of commodities."⁴³ Every opportunity is taken to make use of every animal part; if there are parts left over, they are made into foods that are preserved to be eaten later. Sport hunting is considered wasteful, and unacceptable to *nêhiyaw* people. The idea of avoiding waste extends in at least some instances to limit kills to what is needed by the hunter and his dependants in the short term.⁴⁴

ohcinêwin does not exclusively apply to hunting. Other elements such as over-harvesting of trees, polluting the environment, and various acts that harm all of creation are included. When Treaty 6 was negotiated, the leadership of the day expressly demanded prohibiting the free use of poison (strychnine):⁴⁵ it has almost exterminated the animals of our country, and often makes us bad friends with our white neighbours.⁴⁶ The chemicals used and the effects of corporations harvesting various resources from the territories of Indigenous peoples has historically been of great concern to *nêhiyaw* people. This is expressed time and again in the literature on the subject. It stems from these laws of *pâstâhowin* and *ohcinêwin*.

A subcategory is *ohcinêmowin*. This is similar to *pâstâmowin*, except this law is directed to all of creation, excluding humans. There is very little known about this human law and very little literature is available. What is known is that humans cannot speak badly or think bad thoughts prior to hunting or after the hunt.⁴⁷ Although *ohcinêmowin* has interchangeably been called *pâstâmowin*,⁴⁸ it is a separate law. Prior to hunting, the gathering of medicines/plants, and activities that involve an interaction with creation, a person prepares days ahead of time. For example, if a person is going to pick sweetgrass, they must first smudge and "clean" their minds of all impure thoughts and actions.⁴⁹ A certain demeanour is expected, after a person smudges, they must not use profanity or inappropriate language while doing the task of picking sweetgrass — even before picking the sweetgrass they must put tobacco down on the ground in a clean place to give thanks.⁵⁰ "Clean" means a place away from human activity. It is a ceremonial activity to interact with creation in some form or other. Permission is always asked from all manner of creation based on the belief that all things have a spirit.

After a law(s) is broken, it needs to be identified. The *nêhiyaw* word for all the human laws is *wiyasiwêwina*.⁵¹ There are laws for murder, stealing, disrespect, dishonouring your relatives, incest, sexual assault — all human actions or inaction that break a law or laws. These are the laws under which Treaty 6 was created and are considered the foundation. Elder Jimmy Myo stated, "you cannot begin to understand the treaties unless you understand our cultural and spiritual traditions and our Indian laws."[52] When people from other continents arrived on the shores of North America, First Nations laws, protocols, and procedures set the framework for the first treaties among Aboriginal peoples.[53] We have laws as Indian people and those laws are not man-made, they were given to us by God.[54]

The *nêhiyaw* recount the creation of man and woman, the first *pâstâhowin*, the first prayer, and the first *ohcinêwin*.

> Long ago after the human beings were created, they were allowed to walk with the animals and talked amongst each other like relatives. Even the trees, plants, all manner of life was able to communicate with each other. The was the beginning of understanding *wâhkôtowin* and the laws surrounding it. However, the animals and human beings broke this law, as a result the life-giver took away the ability to speak to each other as punishment. We still remember we are related to all of creation, that is still followed to this day.[55]

Everything has a beginning and each beginning is a gift from the Creator.

One of the foundational laws that developed the treaty interpretation is *miyo-wîcêhtowin*. No relationship could be developed without the *nêhiyaw* law of *miyo-wîcêhtowin*, meaning "having or possessing good relations."[56] *miyo-wîcêhtowin* originates in the laws and relationships that their nation has with the Creator:[57]

> It asks, directs, admonishes or requires Cree people as individuals and as a nation to conduct themselves in a manner such that they create positive good relations in all relationships.[58]

The root of *wîcêhtowin* is *wîcêw-* which means to come alongside or to support.[59] It is this *nêhiyaw* law and others which are the foundation for Treaty 6. Each party applied its own laws to reach an accord.[60] Even among themselves, the *nêhiyawak* followed this law. In all of the established home sites, the Crees lived at peace with one another.[61]

Other laws such as *nipahtâkêwin* (murder), *kimotiwin* (stealing), *ohpikinâwasowin* (child rearing/raising), *nipahisowin* (suicide)[62] are defined and understood in the *nêhiyaw* legal systems. If an individual committed murder, then they have committed *pâstâhowin*. The physical act of killing a human being is subjected to the scrutiny of *pâstâhowin*. However, if a person were to utter "death threats" or "death wishes," then they are subject to the law of *pâstâmowin*. Even thinking of committing murder is contrary to the mental gift.

Finally, the seven pipe laws direct the *nêhiyawak* to lead a life based on these laws. They are understood to be in the following:

> However, most believe that the Sacred Pipe has seven Pipe laws that
> are followed by the carrier and all who are participants or observ-
> ers in the Pipe ceremony. The Pipe laws include "health, happiness,
> generosity, generations, quietness, compassion and respect." The
> Pipe carrier is expected to follow the Pipe laws in their own lives.
> They are held at a higher standard than other individuals because of
> these laws.[63]

Elders have also added another law to this, and this is the person's power, the gifts that the person may have earned during a vision quest or by other means. The Jesuits who noticed strong ceremonial connections also commented on the social ethic calling for generosity, cooperation, and patience, and Le Jeune [a Jesuit] commented on the good humour, lack of jealousy, and the willingness to help that characterized daily life.[64] Those who did not contribute their share were not respected, and it was a real insult to be called stingy.[65]

Indigenous laws are told in life stories that have been passed down from generation to generation; soon the names fade, but the moral and ethical elements remain.

> *kayas* (a long time ago) an old woman heard a young man gos-
> siping to his friends so she took him aside and said, "Come and help
> me pluck the ducks for supper." The young man said yes. As they
> plucked the feathers, the old woman told him, put the feathers in a

bag, so he did. After they were done, she took him to a hill where there was wind blowing on their backs. She said to him, "Throw the duck feathers into the wind." The young man threw the feathers into the wind; as expected, the wind carried the feathers a long distance, spreading them everywhere as the young man and the old woman watched. After a while, the old woman told the young man, "Now, I want you to go and take back every feather you've thrown into the wind and bring it back to me." The young man spent almost all day picking the feathers. After a while, he returned to the old woman and said, "I can't pick every feather, it's impossible because I don't know where the wind has carried the feathers." The old woman told the young man to sit down. The old woman said to the young man, "When you gossip and spread information that is not true, it's like those feathers: you don't know where your words have gone and to take back what you say is nearly impossible."

Gossip is breaking one of our Creator's laws, simple as that. Especially when a person carries a pipe. We all have a responsibility to behave and speak honourably and gently to our fellow human beings.

— Juliette McAdam Saysewahum

The remedies to address the broken laws are diverse and many. These remedies can be found in the ceremonies and activities of the *nêhiyawak*. However, much of the literature is based on European understandings and worldviews, and have come under criticism for that reason. Dr. Waziyatawin Angela C. Wilson explains:

American Indian history is a field dominated by white, male historians who rarely ask or care what the Indians they study have to say about their work. Under the guise of academic freedom they have maintained their comfortable chairs in the archives across the country and published thousands of volumes on whites' interpretations of American Indian History. Very few have attempted to find out how Native people would interpret, analyze, or question the documents they confront, nor have they asked if the Native people they

are studying have their own versions or stories of their past.[66]
Long before any Europeans walked the territories of the *nêhiyawak*, crimes
were virtually unheard of. The general lack of quarrelling or interpersonal
conflict in Amerindian communities impressed Europeans, who won-
dered how peaceful relations could prevail without the threat of force in
the background.[67] During the initial meetings of Jesuits and Indigenous
peoples, the Jesuits observed:

> Besides having some kinds of laws maintained among themselves,
> there is also a certain order established as regards to foreign nations.
> Amerindians treated any person caught breaking these rules like
> a thief. They sealed these agreements by an exchange of gifts and
> hostages which led to the formation of blood ties.[68]

The *nêhiyaw* laws are intertwined with the spiritual realm and are animated
by the spiritual teachings and understanding given to them by the Creator.
Every spoken word or act is based on a spiritual connectedness with the
Creator; living by the laws of the *nêhiyaw* Nation is a way of life, lived daily
through prayer and ceremony. The language is just as important: how a
person speaks to other humans, to the environment, to the land, and to the
animals affects the spiritual and physical balance. All these things must be
respected and adhered to or there will be consequences.

An Elder's Teaching

*My brother in kinship is my cousin but he is my brother. He likes his alcohol
and drank much of his life. He also enjoyed going out to the land to hunt and
trap and was a skilled hunter. About 12 years ago, in the middle of winter . . .
I think it was January, anyway it was very cold. My brother hitched a ride
to the nearest town that was close to his trapline. He planned to go trapping.
He stayed too long at the beer parlour, it was late in the day when he started
down the 10-mile walk on the grid road to his trapline. He was found the next
day frozen to death on the side of the road with his little bit of groceries and
beer. They took his body to the nearby town, to the morgue.*

*It was on the third day, my brother said he woke up. He went to the door
and knocked. The nurse must have been walking by, opened the door. The*

nurse started screaming and she ran down the hallway. My brother said "It was funny the way the nurses ran away from me." He said he was examined by the doctor; the doctor was astonished to see that he was fine.

My brother came back to the reserve. About a month later, he asked us to start a sweatlodge for him. He said he had something to say. This is unusual of him, he hardly ever goes into any ceremonies because he drank too much and had respect for our lodges. When we went into the sweatlodge, my brother told me, "You travel lots and you see many people, I want you to tell them what I'm going to say." He said that the more his message was shared, the easier his journey to the Creator will be.

My brother said, "I was sent back here to tell people something. I drank alcohol most of my life during my time here so I must pay for that." He told us, he had to correct as much as possible the laws that he had broken. Also he was told, he had to share a message. This message was that people were breaking four of the most profound of the Creator's laws far too much, and the people must correct this. These laws are as follows;

1. *gossiping; there are too many people breaking this.*
2. *To have care and compassion for orphaned children.*
3. *not to be jealous of people's successes, their material gains, etc.*
4. *greediness, to be as generous as possible because far too many people have become greedy.*

My brother said this message needs to be told and shared, not only to help him but there are consequences when we do not follow the Creator's laws. My brother was not long for this world shortly after that, he was with us maybe another two years when the Creator took him again. My brother told me to share this experience with as many people as possible because he was sent back from the spirit world to share it. My brother drank too much when he was with us so he was sent back to talk about this, it was a way to "pay" for his pâstâhowina. *He was told, the more people share his story and learn from it, his journey to the spirit world will be easier and peaceful. I hope that people will share and learn from his experience,* êkosi.[69]

b. *nikamona* (songs) to call the Animals: A Hunter's Teachings

The *pîwaya* floating in the air signal preparation for hunting.[70] The land most certainly "speaks" to the hunters, letting them know that the animals are fat and are "ready" to be hunted. The preparations are as ancient as the songs and the land itself. It is no easy task to hunt animals because hunting is a spiritual and ceremonial task. The ceremony varies from nation to nation, but the core aspects are similar.

As stated above, *ohcinêwin* means "the breaking of a law(s) against anything other than a human being"[71] and *ohcinêmowin* are the foundation to hunting and to all aspects of creation.

nêhiyawak understand that all of creation has an *ahcahk*,[72] meaning spirit or soul. Most Algonquian speakers conceptualize animals and sometimes plants with a certain *manitow* (or force) and consider them a "separate nation."[73] For example, an Elder describes this understanding through a teaching expressed to *nêhiyaw* children:

> The birds and the eggs in a nest have been given a way to survive
> and to live. A human being is not allowed to bother or to touch the
> nest nor the bird. The nest is the bird's home, the eggs its children,
> they too have been given something sacred from the Creator and
> that is life. How would a human being react if their home was dis-
> rupted and their children harmed in any way? The animals are to be
> given the same respect for their children and for their homes. This
> applies to all creatures, human life, and the earth.[74]

Each of these plant nations, animal nations, and water nations must be respected equally. To do less is to break the law of *ohcinêwin* and *ohcinêmowin*, depending on what the action is.

The understanding of the *nêhiyawak* about all of creation is animated with spirituality and a connection to the spirit world rooted in a deep respect for spiritual laws. Indians, it is said, were and are conservationists of wild resources; with respect to animals, "conservation" means variously limiting kills to what is needed for survival, utilizing all products of the slain animal, and managing animal populations on a sustained yield basis.[75] An example of this sacred method of conservation is evidence that the *nêhiyaw* hunters did not kill pregnant animals.[76]

Another term utilized to describe the relationship the *nêhiyaw* have with creation is geopiety.[77] This term describes the renewal ceremonies conducted in a specific location and which could not be transported.[78] The ceremonies renewed and affirmed the ancient family relationships to the land, symbolically asserting and adjusting claims to the ecosystems. The responsibility to care for and adhere to the *nêhiyaw* laws of the land with its ecosystems fell to the family. This included specific laws on how to hunt the animals.

omâcîw nikamona means hunter songs. Hunters of the *nêhiyaw* Nation have sung these songs since ancient times, beyond the memory of humans. Cree hunting songs are one subset of a more inclusive group of songs whose performance is associated with communication with the spirit beings and typically also with a positive influence on some objective desired by the singer.[79] The objectives vary from praying for a successful hunt to thanking the animal who sacrifices its life so that the hunter can provide for his family. Crees say that both the music and the lyrics of sacred or magical songs originate in dreams, the singer either learning them in a dream experience or composing them to commemorate one.[80]

The lyrics can invoke the spirit of the wolf so that hunter will be like a predator,[81] hoping "that he would be, like a wolf, a good and successful hunter."[82] During this time of singing and praying in preparation for the hunt, great care is taken to utter[83] language to influence a successful hunt. The law of *ohcinêmowin* prevents hunters from using profanity or boasting before and after a hunt.[84] Any inappropriate verbal act that is contrary to *ohcinêmowin* will bring repercussions of some kind either by the animal not returning or diminishing; therefore, the hunter will struggle to feed his family.

There are ceremonies in place to guide the hunters for the various seasonal hunting patterns so that no laws will be broken. However, if a law is broken, ceremonies are sought out immediately to repair and correct the broken law. For example, if a hunter accidentally killed a pregnant deer, a ceremony is done to ask for forgiveness from the spirit of that animal.[85] The breaking of *ohcinêwin* and *ohcinêmowin* was so rare that instances of forceful coërcion occurred during communal bison hunts when individual transgressions of hunting codes were punished by members of the warrior society.[86]

These laws are still practiced today in many hunts. However, it's become difficult and challenging to hunt, gather, and fish when the lands are being devastated by extractive industries that affect the health of land, animals, and water. Many knowledge keepers and Elders maintain that Indigenous peoples are the stewards and keepers of the land. It's contrary to *nêhiyaw* laws to remain silent about ongoing devastation. The ceremonies continue and the songs carry on much of the knowledge about the laws.

c. Braiding Our Mothers' Hair: It's Time to Bring the Ceremonies into the Daylight.

The songs of the *okihcitâwiskwêwak* have been silent a long time. Occasionally, for those women who have carried the knowledge of ceremonial song, they will sing to recall the teachings and to remember the authority and power Indigenous women once had. This respect for women is evident in the languages of First Nations. The word "fire" in *nakawê* is defined as a "woman's heart." They say that the love of a woman is so great that it caused creation to take place, and, because her love is so powerful, when she withdraws it, destruction can occur.[87] *nêhiyaw* women are the law keepers as well as knowledge keepers of the principles and customs of their people. The women who were chosen for these roles were called *okihcitâwiskwêwak*.[88]

Very little is known about this particular group of *nêhiyaw* women, but they did play a significant and vital role for their nation. To translate the term *okihcitâwiskwêw* is difficult; the closest translation in English is clan mother/warrior woman.[89] *okihcitâwiskwêw* is singular, but if one is speaking of more than one *okihcitâwiskwêw* then the -*ak* is added at the end to pluralize the term.

Historically, women had various roles; some are easily identifiable, and others are interrelated and vary from nation to nation. However, it is generally agreed that women did have authority and power in their respective nations:

In many Aboriginal nations, women could become warriors, hunters, healers or bearers of chiefly names and titles. But their contribution to the well-being of the community was typically through responsibilities specific to women, including marriage and child rearing. The fact that women did so-called women's work did not necessarily mean that they had minor influence or low status.[90]

The *okihcitâwiskwêwak* had specific duties within the *nêhiyaw* Nation. Their influence and authority placed them as advisers to the *okimâw* (chief) and his headman. The structure of *nêhiyaw* governance is critical to examining where the lodge of the *okihcitâwiskwêwak* is placed.

This is an account told to an elder in which the *okihcitâwiskwêwak* gathered together for the last time in the memory of the people:

> Four generations ago, the *okihcitâwiskwêwak* had their last ceremony north of my people's reserve. They gathered together and they built the sundance lodge. It was all women who did the work. They carried the *okimâwâhtik* on their shoulders and brought it to the lodge. The helpers to the *okihcitâwiskwêwak* were called *kâ-omîkwanisicik iskwêwak* (the feathered women), the callers were called *câcikwêsîsak*. The sundance lodge was smaller but similar to the lodges used today. The women had their drums but they are not the same drums used today. The women sang the ceremonial songs, the women helpers knew their duties. Those days, women had their own drums but these drums were gifted to them from the "little people"; such was the power of women during that time. The women drums had strings with humming bird feathers attached at the ends.[91]

The ceremonies were conducted during the day and were never done during the night. Many people have forgotten that when the ceremonies were made illegal by the *Indian Act*, many of them had to be done at night, but now it's time to bring them back into the daylight.

During and prior to treaty making, it would have been the *okihcitâwiskwêwak* who would have been consulted regarding the land, because authority and jurisdiction to speak about land resides with the women. The water ceremonies belong to the women. Very little is written or known about this, other than that their connection is based on the understanding that the earth is female and the authority stems from this.

The criterion to become an *okihcitâwiskwew* is strict and sacred. Most are "born into" this role or are later identified and raised in the teachings and knowledge. Usually there are nine *okihcitâwiskwêwak*, but seven deal with matters of everyday concerns. The other two are not called upon unless the incident is serious and needs their attention.

The criterion itself is based on knowledge, teachings, and ceremony. The women would be raised to become "doctors" or shamans.[92] They must have extensive knowledge about the plants of the land and their uses; generally this knowledge is utilized in a ceremony called the *mitêwiwin (midewin)*.[93] The women must be gifted with various ceremonies and their knowledge must be quite extensive. Their primary knowledge would be the laws of the people. If a law is broken, the *okihcitâwiskwêwak* would be summoned. The law breaker would be brought before the *okihcitâwiskwêwak* to answer for his or her deed.

The power and authority of women was reflected in every aspect of the nation's activities. As the Jesuit Paul Le Jeune stated,

> The choice of plans, of undertakings, of journeys, of winterings, lies in nearly every instance in the hands of the wives. The women have great power here. A man may promise you something but if he does not keep his promise, he thinks it is sufficiently excused to tell you his wife did not wish it.[94]

Further:

> the woman was defined as nourisher, and the man, protector, and as protector, he had the role of helper. He only reacted: she acted. She was responsible for the establishment of all the norms — whether they were political, economic, social or spiritual.[95]

The sacred tasks and jurisdiction of the women persist. Although colonization has taken a toll, it does not extinguish nor diminish their jurisdiction and authority.

Much of the way of doing things may have diminished; however, the markings, songs, and lodges of the women expressed and renewed their power and standing. The *nêhiyaw* women painted themselves with bright colours;[96] this either reflected their role within the nation or the designs were imparted in a vision to the dancer or to the one who painted the design.[97] These designs are usually located in a visible area such as the arms, face, or legs.

nêhiyaw women enjoyed the protection of the men; their freedom was unparalleled in a time when the people exercised a freedom that the Europeans described as a utopia. The men would kill to protect the women during this era.[98]

During the treaty making process, colonization and genocide had already taken a toll on many *nêhiyaw* nations. Many of the *okihcitâwiskwêwak* by this time were "hidden," their ceremonies taken deep into the forests of their territories. It was in the lodge called *okihcitâwiskwêwikamik* (clan mother/warrior woman lodge) that a ceremony was conducted during the treaty making process.[99] The *okihcitâwiskwêwak* knew that the land was going to change and that their decisions would affect generations to come. The men informed the *okihcitâwiskwêwak* of the negotiations and what decisions must be made.

A ceremony was conducted for four days and four nights asking the *âtayôhkanak* (spirit keepers) what must be done. During this time the women prayed and some fasted, as is the custom. An understanding was made and was taken to the men. This understanding is explained further in chapter four.

Further, during the ceremony *âtâyohkanak* entered the lodge of the women. There were many who entered but five made a declaration. The first *âtayôhkanak* that came was *pîsim* (the sun). The sun told the women, "I will bear witness to this exchange and I will stand by it for all time." The second and third *âtâyohkan* was the *nipiy* (water), but it was the male and female *nipiy* that came in and they, too, stated, "We will bear witness to this exchange and we will stand by it for all time." The fourth *âtâyohkan* was the *wîhkask* (sweetgrass); the grass told the women, "I too, will bear witness to this exchange and I will stand by it for all time." The final *âtâyohkan* was the grandfather rock, who stated, "I too, will bear witness to this exchange and I will stand by it for all time." The grandfather rock is the pipe used to seal the exchange in what is now considered a covenant.

This is why the term "as long as the sun shines, the rivers flow, and the grass grows" from the numbered treaties is so important and critical. The ceremonies of the women involved much more than singing and dancing;

decisions and laws were carried, discussed, and applied. The power and authority still resides with the women, especially the *okihcitâwiskwêwak*, in matters of lawful decisions and remedies.

Much of the historical literature seems to exclude Indigenous women, in particular *nêhiyaw* women. The Royal Commission on Aboriginal Peoples had this to say:

> The historical and traditional roles of women has been varied and poorly recorded; although even those that are recorded are of concern. These records are problematic because they were generally written by non-Aboriginal men —fur traders, explorers, missionaries and the like. Regrettably, the views of Aboriginal women were often not recorded. What was observed by European settlers were the power Aboriginal women enjoyed in the areas of family life and marriage, politics and decision making, and the ceremonial life of their people. It has been noted that the Jesuits, steeped in a culture of patriarchy, complained about the lack of male control over Aboriginal women and set out to change that relationship. The change was drastic and detrimental to Indigenous women, the effects felt in the generations to come.[100]

The power and authority the Jesuits witnessed during that era are now a mere shadow for many Indigenous women throughout Turtle Island (Canada). Colonialism and genocide have sabotaged the role of women and reduced them to second-class citizens in their own nations. This is evident by the staggering number of missing and murdered Indigenous women in what is now called Canada. "Indigenous women are going missing and being murdered at a much higher rate than other women in Canada — a rate so high it constitutes nothing less than a national human rights crisis."[101]

The role of *nêhiyaw* women needs to be revitalized. The role of Indigenous women is connected to the lands and waters; they are protectors, defenders, and teachers as well as knowledge keepers. The *okihcitâwiskwêwak* are critical and integral to the nationhood of the *nêhiyawak*; their role cannot be underestimated. In order to bring the laws back, it will take a collective effort to breathe life back into the structures of leadership and way of doing and way of being given to the people to follow for all time.

d. The Gift of Language: Revitalizing *wâhkôhtowin* (kinship)

The *nêhiyawak* believe that language has a spirit. This spirit exists as a means to communicate with the Creator, therefore prayers are believed to be heard and answered. The ceremonial language is different from the "everyday" language. The gift of the *nêhiyaw* language is a connection to the Indigenous laws and how imperative these laws are to a *nêhiyaw* way of being and knowing.

This section will emphasize the importance of language and how *wâhkôhtowin* (kinship) is critical and necessary to the foundation of nationhood. The *nêhiyawak* are part of the Algonquian speaking order, and share much of the same understandings and structures as others in their language group. The *nêhiyawak* refer to themselves as a *nêhiyaw*, but they have also been referred to as First Nations, Aboriginal, Indigenous, Cree, and Native.

Colonization and genocide have had a terrible effect on the *nêhiyawak*. Many struggle to relearn their cultures and languages. Elders have lamented the loss of language as more and more young Indigenous people prefer the use of the colonizer's language. The *nêhiyaw* language is said to be "a spiritual gift":

> It was given to us by the father of all. The Indigenous language and that spirit gift, it is ours to use every day as the people that we are. And if we do not speak our languages, that spirit gift goes elsewhere because we reject as it was given to us by the father of all. This is what I have been told and explained growing up. This I tell them. This is what the old grandmothers told me."[102]

This emphasis on *wâhkôhtowin* is the foundation for the farming reserves created for each family at the time of treaty making.[103] Family is not exclusive to blood kin or to extended family; *wâhkôhtowin* includes adopted family:

> First Nations territory is defined by the speaking of a shared linguistic dialect and kinship. Consistent with their verb-oriented reality enfolded in their language, a process of being with the universe, the Algonquian tenure was and is widely shared, coherent, and

interrelated world-view connecting all things. The continuity and authority of the Algonquian tenure is embodied in a common bond or vision that transcends temporary interests. This bond arises naturally from the fate of being born into a family, community and territory.[104]

This bond arises from the use of kinship terms embedded in the language, identifying the place and role of each person in the family.

The *nêhiyaw* language has extensive and complex *wâhkôhtowin*, or *wâhkôhmtowin*, terms that determine how a person is to be addressed and spoken to. The plains *nêhiyaw* language is the "y" dialect. *wâhkôhtowin* or *wâhkômtowin* are used interchangeably; however, *wâhkôhtowin* is used to described the kinship connections to all of creation, such as the various clan systems that create kinship responsibilities to the animals and to creation in general. *wâhkômtowin* is the blood kinship of human beings.

The terms are based on the female and male bloodlines. For example: the term for my father is *nohtâwiy*[105] and the term for my mother is *nikâwiy*.[106] Both are possessive terms that speak from the first person narrative. These terms are not gender based, so a female or male can call their parent by these terms; however, there are other terms that are exclusive to male and female. The children of the parents must follow certain terms based on the male and female lineage. For example, if the mother has sisters, then her children would refer to each of them as *nikâwîs*,[107] which means "my little mother," because of her female line to the mother. However, if the mother's children were to address her brother, then the term would be *nisis*,[108] meaning "father-in-law." These terms determine how the children will behave around the adults; these terms created appropriate and respectful behaviour that discourages abuse and creates relationship boundaries.

There are strict *wâhkôhtowin* and *wâhkômtowin* laws that are followed by the family:

Strict mother-in-law avoidance was observed; nor could a man speak to his father-in-law except under one condition. If on returning from battle, a man presented his father-in-law with a scalp which he had taken, the taboo is lifted.

A woman was very close to her mother-in-law, but could have nothing to do with her father-in-law. In case of dire emergency, as when a woman wanted to warn her father-in-law of an enemy raid, she might turn her back to him and speak so that he could hear.[109]

This adherence to *wâhkôhtowin* is applied just as easily to the land and to creation. *wâhkôhtowin* included the relationship with the beings that the Creator created:

Among Aboriginal peoples traditionally it has been the responsibility of the family to nurture children and introduce them to their responsibilities as members of society. However, the extended family continued to play a significant role throughout the lives of its members. When a young man went out on the hill to seek a vision of who he was to be and what gifts were uniquely his, it was not because he was preparing to go out into the world and seek his fortune. Rather, he would come back to the camp or the village to obtain advice from his uncles or his grandfather on the meaning of his experience, and his "medicine," or personal power, was to be exercised in the service of family and community.[110]

The term *manâcim* means to show verbal respect to someone, take care verbally. Another term which is similar, *kistêyihtamowin*, is the physical respecting of someone. This supports the physical and verbal laws which apply to how a person acts and how they to speak appropriately following kinship terms and laws. There is the verbal respecting and the physical respecting of kin. The respect shown is dependent on the terms and roles of each family member. An elder's teaching supports this understanding:

This one time an elder said to me, "Do you love your dog?" I said, "Yeah, my dog is a good dog and I love it." Then the elder said, "You can love many things in your life, your vehicle, house, etc. You can love your dog too, but do you respect it?" I was kinda dumbstruck by that question because I always thought love and respect blended together. When I really started to think about it, they are two different things. I've had people declare to love me and called me a soul mate but 3-5 days later they're with someone else, likely saying the same thing. When you respect all of creation and humankind, love takes on different meanings and actions. Love and respect are understood differently by my people; respect has two terms, one is verbal and the other is physical. So the question here would be, "You can love something or someone BUT do you respect them?" When you respect something or someone, your actions begin to change. I think it's important that we all begin to understand this in all of our relationships.[111]

There are words or utterances that cannot be translated into English, such as *mahti*. "The particle *mahti* resists translation; it occurs in conversation to preface directives or proposals for joint activity: '*mahti anima mîtawîtân maskokâcôsîwin*' '*mahti* let's play that bear hunt game'.[112] In spiritual or magical speech, '*mahti*' occurs with verbs in future tense to indicate a projective state of affairs desired by the speaker."[113]

Another such word for which is difficult to find a singular English translation is *ê-nipiskêt*.[114] This single word describes a *nêhiyaw* healer going to the spirit world to retrieve a soulflame of a person brought to them who was deceased.[115] Spirit retriever may be the closest translation; however, even that limits the word and does not describe the journey into the spirit world.

There are difficult kinship terms as well, such as *niciwâmiskwêw*, which translates into "other me." This is a female term applied to a woman who is in a spousal relationship with a man and that man's ex-wife would use that term to describe each other.

Syllabics are the written language of the *nêhiyawak*. There are disputes as to the origin of syllabics; according to written history, Rev. James Evans is credited with this ingenuity.[116] According to *nêhiyaw* oral history, the origins of syllabics came from a *nêhiyaw* named Calling Badger. Oral tradition reveals that Calling Badger had died and gone to the spirit world only to come back and to share this written language with his people.[117] There is a similar oral history shared by other *nêhiyawak* such as Montana.[118] Despite this dispute, syllabics was utilized by the *nêhiyawak* but with the advent of the written word, it has fallen to the wayside. There are still some speakers who utilize syllabics, but not as much.

Language and *wâhkôhtowin/wâhkômtowin* are critical and crucial in understanding how *nêhiyawak* regard relationships as the foundation to their ties to everything, including creation. As described in chapter 5, even the land base and territory are determined through family.

Further, it is believed that language heals and the memory of language is carried in the bloodlines of *nêhiyawak*. This memory is carried through the generations by the blood that flows in their bodies and is transferred to their children. Therefore, even before the child is born it is understood they carry sacred bloodlines.

Finally, the colonization of the *nêhiyawak* language deserves a mention. The *nêhiyaw* elders lament the use of certain words that are inappropriately applied to describe European situations or institutions. Words such as *otêkwêwak* mean those persons who are born with the female and male genital characteristics, also known as intersexual persons,[119] which can be translated to mean two-spirited. Another word is *ôtênaw* which is taken from the original word *ê-ôtênawihtàcik*, when translated means "a place or lodge of spiritual people."[120] *ôtênaw* is now used to describe European cities or towns, which is not accurate. Further, *simâkanisak* means "protectors that surrounded the living area";[121] however, this word has been used to describe the European police system, which again is not accurate.

In summary, language is critical in understanding the spiritual, verbal, emotional, and physical way of *nêhiyaw* being. It is also said language carries a "vibration" that connects it to the Creator's creations; thus, the singing and almost a humming sound while in a prayer state. This vibration is a connection to all spiritual things, including the universe. In order to understand *wâhkôhtowin*, the kinship terms provide the foundation toward respectful boundaries, a law to prevent inappropriate actions, behaviours, and attitudes. All of *nêhiyaw* relationships are based on these understandings and laws that must be followed as the foundation to understanding relationships with blood relatives as well as the relationship with all of creation.

CHAPTER FOUR

The Promised Land

The song of a Cree warrior as he prepares for battle:
"I shall vanish and be no more. But the land over which I now roam
shall remain and change not."

— Alphonse Little Poplar[1]

kikâwînawaskiy provides for *nêhiyaw pimâcihowin*

AS THE *NÊHIYAW* PIPE IS RAISED, voices can be heard humming in a low
monotone as prayers are said by the group gathered. Always since the Creator put the *nêhiyawak* to walk and prosper in their lands, each time the
pipe is lifted in a different direction it is a sacred act. Central to the First
Nations belief systems were sacred ceremonies that gave them access to the
Creator and his creation.[2] The pipe was one of the mediums used to ground
the vows made to the Creator.[3] These vows are to follow the laws of land
and creation.

Resources, environment, and land are critical and essential to the
nêhiyawak, because without these elements, Indigenous culture and
pimâcihowin (livelihood) would not exist. Without land and culture, the
nationhood may diminish for the *nêhiyawak*, perhaps diminishing their
sovereignty. The earth and land are called *kikâwînawaskiy*, meaning mother earth.

In order to understand treaty interpretation, one must understand
the language and culture, and know the lands. For Treaty 6 territory, and
similarly for all the numbered treaties, two significant things occurred.
pimâcihowin (livelihood) split two ways: the livelihood that existed prior
to treaty making and the livelihood that was created by treaty making. Although agriculture was practiced by Indigenous people before European

contact, this specifically speaks to the European method of agriculture. Indigenous economy did exist in terms of trade, a form of gambling, and other forms of economy that won't be discussed here. The primary focus for this chapter is agriculture.

The *pimâcihowin* that existed prior to European contact consisted of sustenance and an economy shared with other Indigenous nations from the land as given to the *nêhiyaw* people by the Creator. This inherent *pimâcihowin* respected the land through the law of *ohcinêwin* and *ohcinêmowin*, which prevented and limited activities that may harm the environment, land, and all of creation:

> When you go out to gather medicine you must prepare yourself with prayer and cleansing, otherwise the medicine will hide from you. When you find the medicine it will be growing in families and you must leave the babies because they are the next generation. You must be careful to gather both the male and the female, otherwise your medicine will have no power. When you collect water to prepare the medicine you must dip your bucket with the flow of the stream. Otherwise your medicine will have no power.[4]

The "bundle" of laws which *pimâcihowin* carries are inextricably tied to *ohcinêwin* and *ohcinêmowin*. Understanding and knowing the use of each plant, animal, and sacred site animate each act in reverence for creation. The Elder in the above statement shares that all creation has a female and male self. If a person does not know this about creation, then they are liable to pick the wrong plant; for example, in health matters concerning women, this requires picking of female plants. It would be an inadvertent *ohcinêwin* if male plants are harvested when a person does not have the knowledge to pick the right plants. However for illnesses that are not specifically male or female, then combining male and female plants is acceptable.

As discussed in the previous chapters, the law of *ohcinêwin* is applied to land but is not limited to it. Protocol is important at the beginning of each undertaking when a person requires something from the lands, be it waters, plants, animals — all of creation. Tobacco would be put in a clean place to thank the land for providing the plants, trees, animals, and for all of creation. Part of protocol in following the law of *ohcinêwin* is to put tobacco offerings before picking medicines or anything from the land.[5] In some instances, if it is a specific, powerful healing plant, certain ceremonial requirements must be met. If these requirements are not met properly or are not done at all, then the plant will not return, and this would be considered bad luck.[6] This form of land and environment understanding has been referred to as "sacred conservation."[7]

Agriculture in varying stages was practiced by the Indigenous people all over Turtle Island (now called Canada and United States). The people who hunted on the northwestern plains harvested plants such as the prairie turnip, which they had to observe carefully to determine the right time to gather it for drying and pulverizing for winter use.[8] The "new world" domesticated plants that have made the largest contribution to world agriculture were all of undisputed American origin, developed by Amerindian farmers.[9] Historians referred to the Indigenous people of Turtle Island as Amerindians in the early eras of history. Indigenous plants included tomatoes, peanuts, pineapples, cacao (from which chocolate is made),[10] sunflowers, corn, squash, various varieties of maize, 30 varieties of wild fruit and at least 10 kinds of nuts besides other varieties of wild foods.[11]

The lands of Indigenous people also provided plants which are the major source of medicines.[12] Recollect missionaries would report from Acadia, "Amerindians are all by nature physicians, apothecaries, and doctors by virtue of the knowledge and experience they have of certain herbs, which they use successfully to cure ills that seem to us incurable."[13] Amerindians used more than 500 drugs that are still in use today.[14]

Hunting, gathering, fishing, and various other activities are protected under these numbered treaties. Of inherent activities that existed prior to treaty making, it is understood that, "what I offered does not take away your living, you will have it then as you have now, and what I offer now is put on top of it."[15] Indigenous people understood this to mean they would have freedom to access all areas of water and land.

With the buffalo disappearing and the demand for Indigenous lands, concerns were raised many times in the treaty books surrounding livelihood and how the generations to come would sustain themselves. One of the issues raised was to have the buffalo protected for the use and benefit of the *nêhiyawak* as part of the agricultural terms and promises. In fact, the *nêhiyawak* wanted a law passed to protect the buffalo. The governor replied that if such a law be passed it will be printed in Cree as well as in English and French; but what that law will be I cannot tell.[16] However, in Treaty 8, there are references that a law has already been passed to protect the buffalo for the use of the Indians.[17] With agriculture as an alternative to the disappearing buffalo, it paved the way to the another *pimâcihowin*.

The second *pimâcihowin* is the treaty term and promise of lands, agricultural land, and agricultural assistance. At the time of treaty making, most of the lands were surveyed in a similar fashion. However, a review of the other numbered treaties gives insight and direction to the negotiations, along with other sources of information. Historians have noted the inconsistency to the Treaty Commissioner's address to the Ojibwa at the Treaty negotiations with the language used in the written treaties.[18] In fact, concerns were raised about possible fraudulent activities of Indian Agents and the government.

As stated above, the surveying of all reserves were similar with all the numbered treaties. The difference lies in the size of each lot; a review of each numbered treaty will show varying sizes of surveyed land. Several copies of treaty books are available with some slight modification to the wordings: the book by Alexander Morris states, for example, "every family of five a reserve to themselves of one square mile"; whereas the book by Roger Duhamel states "one square mile for each family of five, or in that proportion for larger or smaller families." According to Morris's report:

> We wish to give each band who will accept of it a place where they
> may live; we wish to give you as much or more land than you will
> need; we wish to send a man that surveys the land to mark it off,
> so you will know it is your own, and no one will interfere with you.
> What I would propose to do is what we have done in the other
> places. For every family of five a reserve to themselves of one square
> mile. Then, as you may not all have made up your minds where you
> would like to live, I will tell you how that will be arranged: we would
> do as has been done with the happiest of results at the North-West
> angle. We would send next year a surveyor to agree with you as to
> the place you would like.[19]

The printed version of Treaty 6 reads:

> And Her Majesty the Queen hereby agrees and undertakes to lay aside reserves for farming lands, due respect being had to lands at present cultivated by the said Indians, and other reserves for the benefit of the said Indians, to be administered and dealt with for them by Her Majesty's Government of the Dominion of Canada; provided, all such reserves shall not exceed in all one square mile for each family of five, or in that proportion for larger or smaller families, in manner following, that is to say: that the Chief Superintendent of Indian Affairs shall depute and send a suitable person to determine and set apart the reserves for each band, after consulting with the Indians thereof as to the locality which may be found to be most suitable for them.[20]

These lands are reserved for Indians for their use and benefit, at the time of surveying; the surveyor would have taken into account the number of families. The criterion to "qualify" is based on the one square mile per family of five, or in that proportion for larger or smaller families for Treaty 6.

Each family of five thereafter would have provided for themselves through agriculture and agricultural assistance as promised under the treaty terms. Upon review of what is agricultural assistance, the understanding is varied but similar. In a case called *Beattie* v. *Canada* from Treaty 11, Joyce Beattie wanted agricultural assistance for her residence in British Columbia. The court decided had she been residing on Treaty 11 lands, she would have been eligible for agricultural assistance based on the following statement:

> This undertaking is supported by a commitment on the part of the Crown to provide certain tools and supplies which are useful for hunting, fishing and trapping. However, the possibility that some Indians might wish to abandon their traditional lifestyle is recognized in the promise of assistance to those wishing to engage in agricultural pursuits. The content of the duty to provide agricultural assistance must be derived from the fact of a transition in lifestyle from a nomadic existence, based on hunting and fishing to a more settled

lifestyle which is described as engaging in "agricultural pursuits."[21]

Joyce Beattie was practicing agriculture and was eligible for agricultural assistance; however, it was limited to Treaty 11 lands and not applicable outside those lands — in her case, British Columbia. This is not to say the common law cases are the only means of understanding treaty terms and promises. However, what is missing is Indigenous understanding and interpretation.

Treaty 6 has more specific accounts of what kinds of agricultural implements the family would receive upon taking up agriculture:

It is further agreed between Her Majesty and the said Indians, that the following articles shall be supplied to any Band of the said Indians who are now cultivating the soil, or who shall hereafter commence to cultivate the land, that is to say: Four hoes for every family actually cultivating; also, two spades per family as aforesaid: one plough for every three families, as aforesaid; one harrow for every three families, as aforesaid; two scythes and one whetstone, and two hay forks and two reaping hooks, for every family as aforesaid, and also two axes; and also one cross-cut saw, one hand-saw, one pit-saw, the necessary files, one grindstone and one auger for each Band; and also for each Chief for the use of his Band, one chest of ordinary carpenter's tools; also, for each Band, enough of wheat, barley, potatoes and oats to plant the land actually broken up for cultivation by such Band; also for each Band four oxen, one bull and six cows; also, one boar and two sows, and one hand-mill when any Band shall raise sufficient grain therefor. All the aforesaid articles to be given once and for all for the encouragement of the practice of agriculture among the Indians. . . .[22]

Further, the treaty right to agricultural assistance is set forth in the following statement:

While the Crown's obligation to provide these goods is not labelled "agricultural assistance" in the treaties, it is clear that it is assistance provided to the Indians to enable them to engage in agriculture. It is not inappropriate to treat the type of materials provided as "agricultural assistance" and to conclude that the agricultural assistance to be provided under Treaty No. 11 would be of a similar kind.[23]

Agriculture is clearly a treaty term and promise; the implements, seeds and so forth are provided for when the Indians decide to take up the practice.[24] The treaty terms and promises to agriculture must be read in a contemporary context, meaning the agricultural implements must be in a modern state. In order for a treaty promise to have substance there must be a place to practice it which means the farmer must have land. Which leads into the issue of land.

Throughout the Treaty texts, the *nêhiyaw* and Saulteaux leadership of the day expressed their concern that the generations to come be provided for. As well, the Governor would support the leadership's statements by saying, "I have proposed on behalf of the Queen what I believe to be for your good, and not for yours only but for that of your children's children, and when you go away think of my words."[25] The land is a integral component of the *nêhiyaw* Nation and this is understood that they cannot sell the land to the detriment of the generations to come. This is supported by Elder and hereditary *okimaw* Francis McAdam (Saysewahum) as he states, "Take a handful of earth in your hand, that is how much you own of the land — the rest belongs to the unborn, the generations to come." Chief Sweetgrass stated, "We heard our lands were sold and we did not like it; we don't want to sell our lands; it is our property and no one has a right to sell them."[26] As well, First Nations treaty negotiators were not authorized to extinguish existing collective or family rights within territories established by First Nations jurisprudence.[27] Several references can be found with similar statements.

The generations to come are provided for through the one-square-mile criterion. Ideally, what should have happened and for some reason did not, was the first families who took treaty land allotments or family farms[28] had their lands surveyed as per treaty and every family who took up agriculture were to be surveyed their one square mile, therefore fulfilling the treaty to provide for all generations. These are the reserves that are seen all over Turtle Island based on the first families who took these lands. It should not have stopped there. A *nêhiyaw* Elder stated, "the land is supposed to grow with the people."[29] According to oral history, a 10-mile or 25-mile belt[30] was to be around every reserve to accommodate for the generations to come, each of whom would take up their one square mile. A statement taken from Treaty 2 supports the notion that concerns of population growth were raised, and that reserve land would increase:

> Her Majesty the Queen "agreed and undertakes" to affirm reserves based on a formula of 160 acres per family unit of five that consented to a reserve. The Treaty Commission had also stressed during negotiations that when the reserve became too small, the government would sell the land and give the families a bigger reserves elsewhere.

> The Treaty Commissioners assured the Ojibwa that the treaty would create a viable future livelihood that would "ameliorate" their present condition and future settlement.[31]

There are disagreements on both sides when the issue of a 10-mile belt is raised; Indigenous people state this to be a true treaty term and promise, but the government disputes that it was ever agreed to.

With this in mind, each family would have raised their children on their Treaty farm lots along with the treaty promise of agricultural assistance. Subsequent families thereafter, descendants of the original treaty families, would have been eligible to the one square mile per family of 5 more or less:

> your Great Mother, therefore will lay aside for you "lots" of land to used by you and your children. She will not allow the white man to intrude upon these lots. She will make rules to keep them for you, so that, as long as the sun shall shine, there shall be no Indians who has not a place that he can call his home, where he can go and pitch his camp, or if he chooses, build his houses and till his land.[32]

This understanding of farm family lots to practice their treaty term and promise of agricultural assistance would be consistent with their concerns that the generations to come would be provided for and would be sustained through a new life. In fact, this is "the promised land" for all treaty descendants. The treaty itself can be described as a "living will" and this would be considered a treaty inheritance.

Another historical fact that bears mention is the implementation of the *Indian Act*, which contradicts the understanding of the treaty promises. The *Act* restricted the activities of treaty farmers and, as a result, many could not make a sustainable living for their families through agriculture. Indigenous people were viewed historically as lacking interest in or aptitude for agriculture, a view disputed by Sarah Carter in her book, *Lost Harvests*. Had the *Indian Act* not been implemented to sabotage the agricultural economy of treaty farmers, they would most likely have flourished.

The pattern on which western settlement is based came from a Homestead Policy[34] and those ideas of land lots and settlement were inserted into the treaties. Similar land lots were issued to those Indians who were ready to take up agriculture as a livelihood. These ideas of land lots were not new to the Europeans, they were brought over from their countries, so it is not a surprise that this method of surveying and ideas of agriculture appear in the treaty documents.

Some have questioned how the treaty promise for the one square mile has not been fully implemented. There are several reasons for it. One of the criteria is that these are lots specifically for a family of five; but shortly after Treaty 6 was made and agreed to, the Indian residential schools began to forcibly take children away, making it difficult for families to meet this criterion. Further, disease had taken a toll of many Indigenous nations, leaving much of the land "widowed." Another reason is the pass and permit system which, although it had no basis in law, was fully enforced, basically keeping Indigenous peoples imprisoned in the lands of those families whose first took up agriculture. In time, after much devastation on Indigenous peoples and Indigenous memory, much of this information was forgotten to the advantage of the *Indian Act* which does not speak to this particular treaty term and promise.

Another element to land that bears mention is the Aboriginal Affairs and Northern Development Canada Land Claims Policy (AANDC formerly known as the Department of Indian Affairs) and the Treaty Land Entitlement (TLE) process. There is so much to write about the Land Claims Process that this small general mention will not be able to cover it. In general, there are two types of Aboriginal claims in Canada that are commonly referred to as "land claims": comprehensive claims and specific claims.[35] Comprehensive claims always involve land, but specific claims are not necessarily land-related[36]; Treaty Land Entitlement (TLE) is part of the land claims process. Although these processes have "given" back some land to Indigenous peoples, what Indigenous people have to give up is the issue. Some of the bands have benefitted from the TLE promises and have accumulated land and funds to address issues of land and economic benefits, as well as use of land to deal with the population growth on reserves.

One of the success stories to come out these agreements is the Muskeg Lake Cree Nation. They utilized the Treaty Land Entitlement (TLE) process to develop the urban reserve in the city of Saskatoon. After a series of complex negotiations with three levels of government, an agreement, *Asimakaniseekan Askiy*, was reached and signed on October 1, 1988.[37] Since that time Muskeg Lake Cree Nation has developed buildings and property.

PHOTO COURTESY THE AUTHOR

In the spring of 2012 Cynthia B. Lachance, pictured here, and I were posting signage like this in an effort to prevent the logging that was devastating the hunting lands.

In 1993 they opened the 52,000-sq. ft. McKnight Commercial Centre,[38] with more successful enterprises leading the way, such as Muskeg Property Management Inc., CreeWay Gas Ltd., CreeWay Gas West Ltd., Creek Investments, Jackpine Holdings Ltd., Dakota Dunes Golf Links LP and STC Inc.[39] There are other bands in similar situations.

There are several reasons to criticize Canada's land claim policy and its premises. The policy requires the extinguishment of Aboriginal rights, including Aboriginal title, in exchange for the rights included in the new settlement or agreement, reflecting the surrender provisions of post-Confederation treaties.[40] In a recent decision on June 26, 2014, the Supreme Court of Canada (SCC) recognized that the Xeni Gwet'in Tsilhqot'in People have Aboriginal title to a large part of their traditional territory.[41] This Supreme Court decision was based on previous legal cases written to contain section 35 of Canada's constitution; the SCC set out a legal test for asserting and establishing Aboriginal title in Canada.[42] Most problematic of the points to be taken from this Supreme Court decision is that it is based on the assertion of European sovereignty; the Crown has "Radical or underlying title," thus keeping the racist Doctrine of Discovery alive in Canada.[43] All the case law decisions when it comes to land claims are based on the Doctrine of Discovery.

Despite the *Tsilhquot'in* decision, in September 2014 Canada quietly introduced the first major reform to the land claims policy in 30 years.[44] The reform does not address existing fundamental issues; instead, it will expedite the elimination of Aboriginal rights. The impediment to the energy market's need to "capitalize" on global energy demands is Aboriginal peoples' consitutionally protected title, rights, and treaties.[45] The new strategy to obtain compliance has more than half of the *Indian Act* chiefs sitting at "termination tables" negotiating away Indigenous rights.

According to Assembly of First Nations (AFN) documents, concerns were raised whether the process of land claims was fair and efficient.[46] A task force had been created for a "new relationship" to address land and other issues. It failed, but the document is still considered the bench mark when dealing with Indigenous peoples.

Moreover, Aboriginal women and their concerns are often left out of land claims negotiations.[47] The requisite land use and occupancy study usually focuses on activities traditionally recognized as male, such as hunting, fishing, and trapping. Land claims policy that prioritizes and focuses on large-scale resource development is also male-centred, because most jobs created by this kind of development are taken by men and because it neglects the socio-economic and cultural implications that may dispropor- tionately affect women in the form of disruption of family and social rela- tions.[48] The *nêhiyawak* believe the women have jurisdiction over land and water, which is contrary to the processes of land claims which are primarily male-dominated chiefs — elected according the imposed *Indian Act.*

If success is to be measured in terms of what Indigenous nations have to surrender, then they are a success within the framework of extinguishment of their inherent rights, treaty terms and promises, as well as Indigenous sovereignty. The agreements are based on several factors, namely:

- "The claimant group bears the onus of establishing Aboriginal title";
- "Governments can infringe Aboriginal rights conferred by Ab- original title";
- "As a general proposition, provincial governments have the power to regulate land use within the province. This applies to all lands, whether held by the Crown, by private owners, or by the holders of Aboriginal title."
- "Provincial regulation of general application will apply to exercises of Aboriginal rights, including Aboriginal title land, subject to the s. 35 infringement and justification framework."[49]

For their surrender of sovereignty and nationhood, these terms relegate Indigenous nations into municipal status, contrary to the spirit and intent of treaties and Indigenous sovereignty. That is a heavy price to pay in terms of the generations to come.

Much of the treaty term and promise for a family of five needs to be ex- plored further because the land base for each reserve in Canada would be subject to increase. Indigenous peoples have always maintained that Canada does not have title to the land until these terms and promises are fulfilled to the treaty *nêhiyawak* and for all the other numbered treaties. It would also create a strong agricultural economic base for all Indigenous treaty peoples.

Further, the land base is not limited to just the one square mile; Treaty 6 as mapped is under the jurisdiction and authority of the descendants. Compensation for lands taken up for settlement have yet to be dispersed by the Dominion of Canada or by the successor state of Canada. The belief that Indigenous peoples "ceded and surrendered" is still a disputed statement. Treaty peoples say they never ceded or surrendered their lands and resources. The treaties are unfinished business. The Doctrine of Discovery no longer has legal standing in international discourse and yet Canada still applies it in all its claims in court for its underlying title arguments. It was unacceptable at the time of treaty and is unacceptable now.

CHAPTER FIVE

Rebuilding Indigenous Nationhood

History has shown that Nations of people can survive wars, disloca-
tion, poverty and disease but when a Nation loses its sense of itself
and a connection to its own past — its identity — that Nation is
truly defeated and not long for this world. Our peoples have been
in intensive contact with the Europeans for 400 years, most of those
years embroiled in conflict stemming from European attempts to
change us or to take away what is ours: our lands, our freedom, our
languages, our names. Those of us who are still here should have
learned one thing by now: survival means never giving up.

— Taiaiake Alfred[1]

Rebuilding Indigenous Nationhood:
kihci-asotamâtowin 6 (nikotwâsik)

*The blackfoot scout carries a painted rod with a small bundle made of
hide tied at the top of the rod. The small bundle carried kinnikanik,
"sacred tobacco" to many of the nations. He walks purposefully towards an invisible line and places the painted rod deep into the ground
bordering the* nêhiyaw *territory. Now he has to wait perhaps overnight
as he makes camp nearby. In the early morning, he returns to retrieve
the painted rod. The rod remains but the kinnikanik has been accepted
and is gone. He has permission to cross the* nêhiyaw *territory. It's
understood that, had the kinnikanik remained he would not have had
permission to enter the land, it would have broken a territorial treaty.*[2]

nêhiyaw Nationhood is as old as the land which the nêhiyawak call *kikâwînaw askiy* (Mother Earth). This section will speak to nationhood as understood by the *nêhiyawak*, shaped and animated by *nêhiyaw* laws. As stated in previous chapters, *nêhiyaw* laws are the foundation to everything and are interwoven in every aspect of *nêhiyaw* life. Treaty with the imperial Crown merely affirms the *nêhiyaw* nation standing. It is a way of life.

There are various accounts of the treaty negotiations. It is only recently that Indigenous people themselves have begun to publish and record their treaty understandings through the oral tradition of their people. Disputes regarding the accuracy of oral traditions make it difficult for knowledge keepers of the *nêhiyaw* nations to bring forward their perspectives. Nonetheless, evidence of the accuracy and credibility of oral tradition surfaces from various European accounts:

> negotiators had to be very careful about what they said as there are always those present who are charged with keeping every word in mind. Once, a Fort Frances chief repeated to him word for word, what Dawson had said two years earlier.[3]

kihci-asotamâtowin nikotwâsik[4] means Treaty 6 lands and territory of the *nêhiyawak*. During treaty making the *nêhiyawak* understood they were not surrendering nor ceding the land or its resources. This is maintained consistently in discussions recorded with Alexander Morris.[5] It was understood the relationship would be based on alliance.[6] *nêhiyaw* ceremonies were conducted throughout, and the pipe was utilized. The *nêhiyaw* understanding of bringing a pipe ceremony into the discussion is that the pipe laws are the foundation to peace. An Elder of the plains *nêhiyaw* Nation once said, "The bravest man was the man who could make peace, who could carry the *oskiciy* (pipe stem)."[7] This is understood to mean that the greatest achievement a warrior (man or woman) can do is to create peace. Anyone can make war, but peace is a difficult achievement.

There are various documents and legislative acts that affect Indigenous Nations in their relationship with the imperial Crown, such as the Royal Proclamation of 1763, the Doctrine of Discovery, and the *Indian Act*. The history of the *Indian Act* is of particular interest because of its evolution. The *Act* did not begin as an instrument of control but rather as a means of creating military alliances, friendship, and peace, called the Indian Military Policy.[8] The evolution in the Indian policy and relationship with the non-Indian people began in three stages:

> First was the evolution of attitudes in which Indians were seen as a separate and special group which had to be dealt with in a certain way. Second was development of a policy to define and conduct the relationship between the two communities. Third came legislation to reflect both the social and attitudes towards Indians and the policy.[9]

In 1670, the British Parliament passed legislation which placed the conduct of Indian relations in the hands of various colonial governors.[10] The legislation commanded peace and friendship in the name of the British Crown to be extended by all the governors to the Indians because of the increase in settlement upon their lands. The legislation contained later instructions to governors, including the following:

> The main elements of future British Indian policy; a) protection of Indian people from unscrupulous traders, b) introduction of Christianity, later becoming the movement to "civilize" the Indian people, c) an "activist" role for the Crown as a protector of "Indians."[11]

However, the legislation did not take immediate effect, and the primary focus during this era was to regulate and maintain the fur trade as well as suppress liquor activity. For the next 68 years, from 1744 to 1812, the direction of Indian policy was relatively straightforward: to maintain the various tribes as military allies because of uncertain American aggressions.[12]

When the Indian Department was established in 1755 it was considered to be an operational arm of the military.[13] The Indian Military Policy was in place to guide this alliance with the various Indigenous Nations. The political relationship between the British government and Indigenous societies was conducted on a "nation to nation" basis, whereby the Indian Department in effect operated as a "foreign office."[14] This is a very important point. The treaties themselves acknowledge them as nations.[15] By their continued existence, and indeed by their constitutional protection, Canada continues to acknowledge them as nations.[16]

Without the knowledge and consent of the Indigenous nations which the Indian Department served, the direction changed later to one of wardship toward the Indians. This policy of wardship would later be the most destructive instrument of genocide against the people it was supposed to serve. This book will not discuss in detail the effects of residential and industrial schools, the intentional distribution of disease-infested blankets, the decimation of the bison, and the broken terms and promises of treaty. Needless to say, the effects are still being felt in the high incarceration rates of Indigenous people in federal and provincial institutions, poverty, murdered and missing Indigenous women, and high rates of suicide.

At the time of treaty making, a structure was in place that involved selecting an *okimâw* (chief) and his *onîkânîwak* (headmen). Attempts and subsequent removal of this inherent structure led to the passage of the 1869 *Act for the Gradual Enfranchisement of Indians and the Better Management of Indian Affairs.*[17] This *Act* authorized the governor to order the elections of chief and council on a three-year term and to dismiss leaders for "dishonesty, intemperance or immorality."[18] This form of removal undermines the sovereignty of Indigenous leaders and puts in place a system similar to the colonizers' way of doing business, which would arguably be a typology of genocide.

The teaching surrounding *nêhiyaw* boundaries is shared by an Elder, who stated:

> At one time, too, the leaders noticed everything. They even knew when a white person was camping inside the reserve, within the boundaries of the reserve, you know. If a white person was seen camping there, right away they would paddle over and send him out. They really did follow the terms of what they had been promised.[19]

> The people had their own scouts and protectors who monitored the lands. There was always fear of whiskey traders and white men who sold unscrupulous items or liquor. There existed Indian police who ensured the laws were followed.[20]

The status of Indians will eventually, through the structure of the *Indian*

Act, be assimilated into the larger Canadian society. This is aptly described in the following:

> what is happening now is a legislated form of population reduction based on the previous goal of assimilation. The ultimate effect of the legislation, despite changes in official policy with regard to assimilation, is to reduce the number of people the government must be accountable to in terms of protection, treaty obligations, land rights, self-government, and other aboriginal rights, including a whole series of culturally specific programs and services that are provided today.[21]

> More and more the Treaty Indians lament the diminishment of various promises and terms such as the medicine chest clause, education, and housing.[22]

The role of women is largely silent in the European books; however, there are some gems that do surface. It's unfortunate more detail is not available because, according to oral history, the *nêhiyaw* women are the law keepers. Even the oral history is scant because of the impacts of colonization and genocide. However, what is available may be enough to revitalize the role of women. They are part of the inherent structure of leadership and are so important in revitalizing the laws.

Some women argue that the notions of self-determination or self-government will not help the plight of Indigenous people, in particular women and children, because the Canadian state does little in the way of alleviating the situation surrounding poverty and other symptoms of colonialism. The following statement supports this notion:

> Liberation from colonialism will be of no assistance to Aboriginal women, if sexism maintains a colonial relationship between Aboriginal men and women . . . women who object to the exclusion of their interests as women are told that there is no issue; and that the political interests of the First Nations are served by denying women's issues. While male leaders speak for "their people" dissident women's voices are silenced.[23]

Replacing one colonial government for another form of it will likely perpetuate the typologies of genocide. The typologies of genocide are the systems of the colonizer such as justice, education, health, religion, economy, and history. It's critical and crucial to identify the factors leading to the current situation of the *nêhiyawak*. It can be argued that colonization and genocide are still at work in the lives of Indigenous peoples.

Genocide is a new word, but the crime is ancient.[24] The lethal impacts of genocide are the same all over the world, destroying nations, engulfing Indigenous people and leaving them in varying degrees of destruction. The variation of genocide is discussed at length from various sources; most agree that the meaning of genocide is the systematic destruction of a group of people based on race, religion, language, etc. Genocide [is] quite simply the destruction of a human group, as such, whether wholly or in part and by whatever means.[25]

The typologies of genocide have been described as the bureaucratic apparatus of the systems.[26] These current typologies perpetuate genocide and assimilation through the justice systems, child welfare systems, churches, education, and various other systems. For example, the education systems continue to teach that the Doctrine of Discovery is the legal basis for European ownership and claim of Indigenous lands, resources, and air.

As well, these systems contribute to and perpetuate the poverty of *nêhiyawak* through limiting funding of programs offered on reserves; one of these is the child welfare system.[27] Currently, challenges to the funding are being pursued in the tribunals of the Canadian Human Rights Commission with some measure of success. Presently, the apprehension of Indigenous children are in the thousands, and these children are placed in non-Indigenous homes, furthering the diminishment of their cultures and languages. Further, present-day symptomology found in Aboriginal peoples and societies does not constitute a distinct psychological condition, but is the well-known and long-studied response of human beings living under conditions of severe and prolonged oppression.[28]

These days reconciliation is the new word touted to lead the way for Europeans and Indigenous peoples in Turtle Island to renew relationships. However, even as the word "reconciliation" is being discussed, it already raises an issue. The word reconciliation means that the two parties involved did not get along in the past and are now making an effort do so:

To put it simply, before two parties can reconcile they must, at some earlier time, have been conciled; that is, two distinct parties, independent and moving in their own directions for their own reason, meet, share and decide to make their independent ways forward into a single combined effort.[29]

Considering and reviewing the history and continued policies maintained by Canada with respect to Indigenous people, it is a problematic and troubling term. The historical and contemporary policies have been the extermination and extinguishment of treaty and Indigenous sovereignty through legislative policies and colonial laws.

Indigenous peoples and some Europeans argue that in order to achieve true justice and the restoration of Indigenous peoples, it has to be meaningful and based on truth. Justice and truth must be based on the following ideal:

> Without massive restitution made to Indigenous peoples, collectively and as individuals, including land, transfers of federal and provincial funds, and other forms of compensation for past harms and continuing injustices committed against the land and Indigenous peoples, reconciliation will permanently absolve colonial injustices and is itself a further injustice.[30]

To speak openly and truthfully about what happened to the Indigenous peoples who live on Turtle Island, to consider the long view and short facts, the Indian problem becomes a question of right and wrong for justice in its most basic form.[31]

The truth about the doctrine of discovery, *terra nullius*, manifest destiny, and various other instruments used to claim the lands, resources, and air of the Indigenous peoples are based on lies. These lies have perpetuated the theft of what is inherently the *nêhiyawak's* given to them by the Creator:

> Something was stolen, lies were told, and they have never been made right. That is the crux of the problem. If we do not shift away from the pacifying discourse of reconciliation and begin to reframe people's perceptions of the problem so that it is not a question of

how to reconcile with colonialism that faces us but instead how to use restitution as the first step towards creating justice and a moral society, we will be advancing colonialism, not decolonization. What was stolen must be given back, and amend must be made for the crimes that were committed from which all non-Indigenous Canadians, old families and recent immigrants alike, have gained their existence as people on this land and citizens of this country.[32]

Before any reconciliation can begin, the settlers need to understand that part of justice is to "give it back,"[33] which is not to say to leave the lands. "Give it back" means to restore the livelihood, demonstrate respect for what is shared — the land — by making things right through compensation, restoration of freedom, dignity, and livelihood.

Colonialism is very much alive and well. As long as the *nêhiyawak* fight for self-determination, fight to determine their own citizens, fight to have equal funding for their children, then colonization and genocide will continue:

> Colonization is not over for this nation and it is not a relic of the past. People are either still benefiting or are still being victimized by the inherited legacy of Canada's colonial history. There needs to be an opportunity for discussion so that we can come to terms with what being Canadian means to each. Canadians can no longer choose to look the other way.[34]

Equality cannot be based on the definition of "equal to Europeans" but in understanding that equality is recognizing the differences. So long as the misguided conceptions of democracy and equality are used as "weapons" in undermining self-determination efforts of *nêhiyawak*, then the fight will continue.

Nationhood and self-determination are based on the laws, cultures, lands, and languages of nations according to the criteria of international law. To be clear, these terms, nationhood and self-determination, are from the European language; they can still be applied to the situation and circumstances of Indigenous peoples. Overwhelming challenges invade every aspect of Indigenous nationhood, terrible myths such as the Doctrine of

Discovery which is the basis of European claims to Indigenous lands, waters, air, and resources. The European narrative of superiority is steeped in every fabric of Indigenous lives; the most obvious is the *Indian Act*.

The past, present, and future must be paved with *nêhiyaw wiyasiwêwina* and *manitow wiyinikêwina*. That is the purpose of this book, so that the generations of Indigenous and non-Indigenous people who share this land may do so in peace and justice. This justice must be defined with "giving it back" in a manner that gives back the livelihood, gives back the freedom and the truth to be told about colonial history. Maybe, then, Indigenous peoples and non-Indigenous people can breathe life back into the treaty terms and promises, the spirit and intent of Treaty 6 and the numbered treaties along with Indigenous sovereignty which, in turn, will protect the lands, animals, and water based on the concept of sacred conservation.

A Spiritual Realization: An Elder's Teaching.

The man sat forlornly praying, deep in his consciousness he finds a place to pray. The memories of his people's poverty, incarceration, suicide, the unending death after death, the children born into such conditions . . . reverberating in his silent words.

He wept as he remembered the land his people once roamed in freedom . . . the peace and solace evades his people, the nêhiyawak.

As he wept, he calls out to the Creator "why have you forgotten my people, why have you forgotten me?" In the depths of his prayer, the silence is cut with sudden visions of beautiful trees, waters, and animals . . . he felt a vibration, a whisper in his mind that said, "I have not forgotten you, you have forgotten me."

The man saw his people had abandoned the gifts the Creator had given them, the animals to eat, the waters to drink, and land to provide livelihood.

It was then he realized the Creator had always been there.[35]

CHAPTER SIX

Idle No More

"Our history is written in the lands of my peoples."

I SAT WITH MY *NOHKOM* EATING GOPHER SOUP in the quiet of her little house down the road from the house I grew up in on the Whitefish Lake Reserve #118. I was about nine years old at the time when I asked her, "Why do you like gopher soup *nohkom*?" She said, "When we were not allowed to leave the reserve, we couldn't hunt the moose or other animals, we had no choice but to eat gophers or we would die, so now I like how it tastes." So I sat there with her enjoying our gopher soup, not understanding she was referring to the pass and permit system that imprisoned my people for so long in our reserved lands. My brothers and I would hunt gophers for her; my most peaceful memories are connected to the lands and waters. My mother and her people are from Whitefish Lake. My father and his people are from Stony Lake. I have many memories connected to both lands, which begins my story of Idle No More.

The rumble of logging trucks rolling down the Stony Lake road seemed louder this night, enough to wake me from my sleep. I have a little shelter/trailer not far from the main gravel road, kilometres from the main highway. I suppose it shouldn't surprise me that they're hauling out the trees from my people's territory as fast as they could, like thieves in the night. This is where Idle No More began for me; little did I know at the time my resistance had begun.

Like anything, a journey begins somewhere, perhaps even before a person realizes their path, each beginning as unique as the story. Idle No More resistance began long before in different names, different locations through the generations since the arrival of Europeans. My own personal journey began when I was writing a chapter in this book about land. I felt disconnected to my childhood memories out on the lands and waters of my people. I decided to return after a lengthy absence, so leaving the city behind I headed home. It was this seemingly simple decision that set my course of action in motion, forever changing my life.

Returning to the land didn't just mean a physical return; it is also an emotional, spiritual, and mental returning. Reconnecting meant it had to be done through the eyes and words of my people's history and ceremony. Returning meant visiting the graves of my people who were nearly wiped out from disease, starvation, and Indian residential schools. I sat by the graves hearing once again that horrible history in the silence of the forest with only my dad and my uncle's words absorbed into the trees, and the land. There are many graves with small broken down crosses with names long forgotten, only some are remembered by those of my family that sur-

This picture of harvested trees was taken in the summer of 2012, before Idle No More began. It has caused me grief and pain to see all these trees harvested, in violation of our treaty terms and promise of hunting.

vived the Hudson's Bay Company's arrival onto our lands. Even though I knew little of the people who lie buried there, I knew they are of my blood. Time after time, I would go to visit them. This is our history, our history began long before the Europeans came here and it will be there long after I am gone.

To summarize some information, my dad Francis McAdam (Say-sewahum) is a hereditary *okimâw* (chief/leader) in a long line of leaders before any European stepped on our lands. Our first treaty *okimâw* is buried in the lands that we are protecting from the extreme logging activities happening even as I write this book. We have done all that we could to get these lands back, with very little resources; it is still in the hands of the colonizer. My people's lands are beautiful. It is in those places that I find my greatest strength, peace, and solace.

Through the spring and summer of 2012, I explored a vast area, often camping in various places. I would find old cabins which would trigger sadness and loneliness but at the same time an interest for the abandoned hunting equipment and glimpses of a past life immersed in Indigenous knowledge as I took pictures of old sweatlodges and wood stoves. Sometimes I would fall asleep and dream at those cabins and lands.

Stony Lake is incredibly beautiful and serene. I remember my father taking us there to swim when we were children. I noticed many changes. I went looking for freshwater streams I had remembered when I was young, often dragging one of my parents with me to search them out. We found many of them were gone. Little by little my heart began to break, realizing the land and waters had changed. It was this change that I began to question.

All these thoughts and feelings kept leading me to continue exploring. While I was exploring I began to feel a profound connection that I can only describe as "falling in love." As a lawyer, it's difficult to bring this revelation for all to read. Love and law in one sentence is not done. Have you ever fallen in love? Then you'd know and understand the feelings of euphoria, attachment, connection, profound and intense affection. The need to be around the object of your love so deeply entrenched in your soul; these are some of the symptoms of falling in love. It's the only way I could describe how I felt that summer. I fell in love with the lands and waters. It was transformative but at the same time an old feeling I still remember from childhood.

Not only did I see the beauty of the lands and waters, I also began to see the devastation of logging and other activities that were happening. I felt grief for the devastation and development I was witnessing; I began to feel a profound and protective love for the lands in which my people were buried and have hunted since time immemorial.

Soon I had many questions that led me to the offices of Saskatchewan Environment which I won't detail here; needless to say, the logging of my people's trees will not stop. As it turns out, that was a minor issue compared to what was to come.

Someone tagged me on Facebook about Omnibus Budget Bill c45 in the fall of 2012. At first I was not interested, but I felt this compelling "pull" to review it so I went back and took a second look. I was angry and stunned. Omnibus Budget Bill c45 was going to change the landscape in terms of protection for waters to "loosen protections contained in the *Navigable Waters Protection Act*, weaken the Canada Labour Code, and alter the *Indian Act* in ways nowhere hinted at in the budget."[1] Its title, "budget" bill, is misleading; it "contains several non-fiscal items that won't be, but ought to be, evaluated by the relevant parliamentary committees."[2] To be specific, the "bill is over 400 pages, containing legislative changes for 64 acts."[3] Further, the *Indian Act* would be amended to "allow First Nations communities to lease designated reserve lands based on a majority of votes from those in attendance at a meeting or in a referendum, instead of waiting for a majority vote from all eligible voters."[4] If the "band members" or Indigenous people wanted a say, the onus would be on them to show up at the referendum or meeting.

The audacity of this particular amendment is that the "Aboriginal Affairs minister would be given the authority to call a band meeting or referendum for the purpose of considering a surrender of the band's territory."[5] This gives the minister of Aboriginal Affairs a veto, even if the majority of Indigenous people were to vote "no" to a surrender or a re-designation of land. It also takes away the power of *Indian Act* chief and councils to stop the minister from calling a band meeting or a referendum. Further, the threshold of consent has been lowered to allow for unfair scenarios like if 50 people showed up from a population of 2,000, those 50 could likely give consent on behalf of the population.

The full impacts of Omnibus Budget Bill c45 have yet to be felt; however, it does remove the protection of water in 99 per cent of lakes and waterways. The economic "opportunities" do not take into account the treaty terms and promises. The treaties that are in place have not been fully implemented nor recognized on the "ground." An example of this is the 1784 Haldeman Tract; although it has been argued that it is not a treaty, it's still an agreement about land. It's a strip of land that runs the length (and 10 km each side) of the Grand River from Lake Erie to its source, including lands in the Kitchener/Waterloo region. The Haldimand Tract is central to ongoing land claim struggles to this day.

To date, Omnibus Budget Bill c45 is not the only bill going through the Canadian Parliament that is problematic and questionable. The other bills are as follows:

- Bill C-27: First Nations Financial Transparency.
- Bill C-45: *Jobs and Growth Act, 2012* (Omnibus Bill includes *Indian Act* amendments regarding voting on-reserve lands surrenders/designations), Received royal assent and is now law.
- Bill S-2: *Family Homes on Reserves and Matrimonial Interests or Rights Act.*
- Bill S-6: *First Nations Elections Act.*
- Bill S-8: Safe Drinking Water for First Nations.
- Bill C-428: *Indian Act* Amendment and *Replacement Act* [Private Conservative MP's Bill, but supported by Harper government].
- Bill S-207: *An Act to Amend the Interpretation Act* (non derogation of aboriginal and treaty rights). Second reading.
- Bill S-212: First Nations Self-Government Recognition Bill (private bill sponsored by Senator Gerry St. Germain).[6]

The design of the above-listed bills are set to undermine the sovereignty and inherent rights of Indigenous peoples by focusing on individual rights, legislatively extinguishing treaty and Indigenous sovereignty. This is the "modern legislative framework" the Conservatives promised in 2006, but from the Indigenous perspective, it is a giant step back.[7] Each bill is in varying stages in the Canadian Parliament. To date some have passed into law despite the intense opposition by Indigenous grassroots peoples through the Idle No More movement.

We focused on Omnibus Budget Bill c45 because it was one of the first Bills to enter the House of Commons. It was Omnibus Budget Bill c45 that brought the other women — Jessica Gordon, Nina Wilson, Sheelah McLean — and myself together asking similar questions. Prior to Idle No More, we did not know each other or had very little contact. We realized we had the same concerns, so we made a decision not to stay silent. According to the definition of acquiesce, compliance is consent, which means if a reasonable minded person is silent about matters like Omnibus Budget Bill c 45, then that is considered consent. We had to reach people. Sheelah came up with the idea of sharing this information in a form of a teach-in. Through a series of discussions in a Facebook chat, we planned the first teach-in for Saskatoon on November 10, 2012. We invited as many people as possible to come and hear what Bill c45 was about as well as the other bills. I remember feeling naïve, hopeful, and confident that all we had to do

DESIGN BY AARON PAQUETTE

was let people know, and if we could get a petition going, the bill could be stopped. I'm not sure what the other ladies thought at the time, but these were my own thoughts.

Shortly after that, I made arrangements to talk to Elders in Maskwacis Alberta (Treaty 6); after a lengthy discussion arranged by Mary Morin, they gave us their support and prayers to try and reach as many people as possible. They also said we must use our own laws; we must invoke one of our most sacred and peaceful laws called *nâtamâwasowin. nâtamâwasowin* is a law carried by *nêhiyaw* (Cree) people in times of great threat and crisis. *nâtamâwasowin* means to defend for all human children of the world as well as future generations. Also *nâtamâwasowin* directs us to defend for the children of all animals, plants, water, and the winged ones — every thing in creation that has a spirit. Part of defending is recognizing that we all want freedom, liberation, and justice for our children. In my people's language children are called *awâsisak* which means "glowing sacred flames"; in this we must view future generations as sacred flames that must be protected, loved, and nurtured.

With this information guiding and directing Idle No More, we reached out to people on social media. We were fortunate our call for help was answered by grassroots people. We had hoped to reach people but Idle No More seemed to resonate to all people from many different lands. Through the ensuing months, Idle No More became a global grassroots movement. We tweeted and Facebooked all our events, round dances, and teach-ins. In a matter of a few months Idle No More was trending on twitter as it began to take hold globally. Soon we were connecting all over Turtle Island; our Idle No More calls for action were heard. Idle No More became one of the largest Indigenous mass movements in recent history and sparked hundreds of teach-ins, rallies, and protests across the continent and beyond. What began as a series of teach-ins to educate about and mobilize around the erosion of Indigenous sovereignty and environmental protection has changed the social and political landscape of Canada. The Idle No More movement provides hope and energy to millions of people.

The round dance became a signature act of resistance all through Turtle Island with incredible songs to accompany it. Many young people came forward to show resistance through their poetry, song, and dance. Soon we began to recognize that the voice of grassroots people through Idle No More was powerful and creative. Youtube became flooded with images of round dances all through Turtle Island inside malls, on roads, streets, and many other places of resistance. It was an incredible time. It still is. It was the winter we all danced, even as temperatures reached -40, it did not prevent actions of resistance. Many times I cried as I witnessed and walked with thousands of Indigenous peoples and allies while we carried our flags, signs, and feathers in actions of peace, justice and solidarity. It was beautiful.

The symbol of the hand holding an eagle feather became the emblem of peace, resistance and revolution for Idle No More grassroots peoples; Aaron Paquette provided the artwork that became recognizable globally. There were many artists who created profound and spiritual works and continue to do so as a form of resistance to the ongoing colonization of Indigenous peoples and lands.

Even with all of our resounding "no consent" protests, rallies, and teach-ins, the Canadian state passed almost all the bills aimed at privatizing treaty lands, extinguishing treaty terms and promises, as well as Indigenous sovereignty. Although this was happening in a highly questionable manner in terms of violating constitutionally protected Aboriginal rights and treaty rights, the Canadian state continued to push forward its termination mandate.[8]

However, it has awakened nations of people to their surroundings; questions and information about the environment, treaties and Indigenous sovereignty are posted and tweeted constantly, something that has long been silent. Canadian laws are constantly changing; a gun law was recently repealed after millions of dollars was spent. These bills can be repealed; Indigenous Nations have stated they will not recognize Bill c45 or the other bills. Allies refused to accept Jubilee medals from the Canadian state in support of Idle No More. Many other actions of resistance were done to support, the young people were especially incredible and powerful; we saw this with the Nishiyuu walkers who walked hundreds of miles from their community to Ottawa. I've always regretted not being able to be there when they arrived in Ottawa and what a powerful arrival it was. I watched it on television, I felt such pride and emotion, I also had hope. We always struggled with funds; all of our work was done with people who believed in Idle No More and we had no money. Every bit of work was volunteer and many gave much of their time.

In the meantime, the extraction of Indigenous resources goes unfettered under the guise of "consultation and consent." There is no consent for many communities; there is no recognition of Treaty terms and promises on the ground as they are continuously violated. For Indigenous people, the ceremonies and lodges continue to pray for the healing of the lands and waters.

More and more settler people are recognizing and understanding that, as a people, we cannot continue to devastate the very things needed to sustain humanity: our lands and waters for the generations to come. The vibration of the earth is out of balance. Our human actions and activities have taken us to a situation of crisis and threat to our humanity and creation. Now is the time for the world to reach into that place of a collective profound love and peace for all *awâsisak* and invoke *nâtamâwasowin*. The highest accomplishment for any person in the spirit of warriors is achieving peace for their nation, but an even greater achievement is to create a world of peace for future generations in a manner that sustains a vibration of love that is healing. It is not enough to say "I love children": we are now called upon to take meaningful, peaceful action in times of conflict and destruction, to remember that our defending is layered with collective sacred love of all children.

Idle No More has taken me to different lands and I have met other Indigenous peoples. I had an opportunity to speak at the United Nations in Geneva Switzerland, I declared in my language, "*niya oma nehiyaw, keyapihc oma etahkweyak, moya atoya nimeschikohnanahk*," which translates into "I am Cree, we are still here, they haven't killed us off." While there, I heard other Indigenous people weep recalling the horror and death they are enduring because of their lands and resources. I made a commitment to myself that I would defend the lands and waters to the best of my ability. I do not want to return to the United Nations weeping for my lands and waters. Not only have I come to call many Indigenous people brothers and sisters, I have come to meet inspiring allies and settlers who truly walked with us. I am forever grateful to be a part of this incredible movement.

In the midst of Idle No More, we knew we were watched and monitored by the government; we expected it. I will not go into detail about the sordid events, trolls, and threats we received while protecting and defending Indigenous sovereignty. It happened. Law has always been used as a weapon against those who stand against colonial mechanisms and genocidal practices. Through the midst of Idle No More, the attacks happened in the media, twitter, Facebook, and sometimes we'd get messages through email. I was more disappointed when it came from Indigenous people. I expected it from non-Indigenous people. However, it did not matter, our actions have always been peaceful; Idle No More is about the love of all things. During this time, the Elders told me not to defend myself from the attacks but to remain focussed and to develop skin "seven generations thick." At times, I felt fear, but for that, too, the Elders had advice; they told me to turn "fear into courage."

I also wanted people to know, I'm not an environmentalist, nor an activist — I'm defending and protecting the lands, waters, and creation with whom I've been taught I have a kinship. My relatives are all of creation. I follow the laws of my people to the best of my abilities; it is all I can do.

As a final thought, I thought I'd like to share nine pieces of advice for everyone. This is what I've learned, that I've attributed to what I believe to be success.

1. Walk as if the Creator is physically walking with you by always listening to your inner "voice" that I call the spirit world voice.
2. Have breakfast any time of the day and enjoy it.
3. The earth Elders and okihcitâwak are right, go with their knowledge; believe in the prophecies and Indigenous knowledge.
4. Find solace and contentment, you will need it many times in your journey; I found mine in the lands and waters of my people's territory.
5. Always believe that we can change our communities to be better, even if you are one voice or four. Find your voice and never be silent; whether it be in song, dance, art, poetry — it is your voice of resistance.
6. Always give back; even if it's a loonie to a small child who wants bubble gum.
7. Give up your vehicle and walk; it's a small sacrifice you won't regret.
8. Never stop learning and listening, it's the breath of life. Our breath is the same breath of our ancestors; it is timeless.
9. Find that place of forgiveness, even if it hurts a lot.

Just mix up that order, no one item is more important than the other. It goes without saying, though: always love and forgive your children.

I am forever changed by Idle No More. This journey has not ended; it's still unfolding as I write this. My journey takes me back to my people's lands and waters; it is in the lands and waters that Indigenous people's history is written. Our history is still unfolding; it's led by our songs and drums. By that, I will say let our actions unfold the future. Let us be Idle No More.

A Treaty "check stop" in the middle of January 2013, a demonstration by the descendants of okimâw Saysewahum because of the violation of Treaty 6 terms and promises on the Stony Lake lands.

Glossary of *nêhiyawêwin* Terms

a

ahâw ... pîhtokwêk — an ancient call from the *oskâpêwis* meaning an invitation and permission for all who are attending the event, ceremony or activity to "come in now"

acahk — spirit/soul

acahk iskotêw — a soulflame

acahkwak — souls or spirits of humans

awâsisak — the term used to refer to children, which means "glowing sacred flames"

â

âtayôhkan — spirit keeper

âtayôhkanak — spirit keepers

c

câcikwêsîsak — female ceremonial helpers/callers

ê

ê-nipiskêt — spirit retriever, a ceremonial person who retrieves the soulflame of someone who has died

ê-ôtênawihtâcik — a place or lodge of spiritual people, those who guide people in the encampment *ê-pâstohtêt* — "stepping over" something, transgressing by stepping over

êkosi — done (enough)

i

iyiniw miyikowisiwin — the First Nations laws and gifts, First Nations understandings of Creation and sacred relationships with all of Creation

k

ka-manitowîmot — to call out to the Creator

kayâs — a long time ago

kâ-kwêskapîstawât — "She Who Turns Sitting (toward another)"; grand-mother of Sylvia McAdam (Saysewahum)

kâ-omîkwanisicik iskwêwak — feathered women

kâhte-ayak — Elders

"kêyâpic ôma ê-ihtakoyâhk" — "We are still here"

kiciwâminawak — our cousins (both yours and mine)

kihci-asotamâtowin — the most sacred of Treaties; this is used when speaking about the numbered Treaties

kikâwînaw askiy — the earth and land, or "mother earth"

kimotiwin — stealing

kinanâskomitinâwâw — I am grateful to you all

kinanâskomitinâwâw mistahi — I am very grateful to you all *kinêhiyawêwininaw* — the gift of our Cree language

kistêyihtamowin — the physical respecting of someone

kîsikâwapiwisk — Sits with the Morning sun (female personal name)

kohkom — your grandmother

m

mahti — equivalent to "please"

mahti anima mîtawîtân maskôcâsôsîwin — "Let's play the bear-hunt game" (Woods Cree)

manâcim — to show verbal respect to someone

manitow — Creator or spiritual life giver

manitow iskotêw — Creator's flame

manitow wiyinikêwina — Creator's laws

maskwacîs — means Bear hills, a name Hobbema has officially changed to

minâtahkâwa — Cypress Hills

mitêwiwin — a medicinal ceremony

miyo — good

miyo-ohpikinâwasowin — good child-rearing or raising

miyo-wîcêhtowin — having or possessing good relations

mîkiwâhp — tipi

mîtawâkîw pisiskiwa — "playing with animals in a bad way," to torture animals, creation — to be cruel (Woods Cree spelling)

môniyâwak — a name given to non-Indigenous people

"môya âtoya nimêschikohnânâhk" — "They haven't killed us off"

n

nakawê — Saulteaux person; of the Saulteaux

nakawêwin — Saultyeaux language

nâtamâwasowin — a law carried by *nêhiyaw* people in times of great threat and crisis that means to defend for all human children of the world as well as future generations

nêhiyaw — a human being or Cree person

nêhiyaw isîhcikêwi — Cree culture/way of doing things that is profoundly connected to mother earth

nêhiyaw kêhtê-ayak — Cree Elder (male or female)

nêhiyaw pimâcihowin — Cree way of living and earning, economics, livelihood

nêhiyaw wiyasiwêwina — Cree human laws

nêhiyawak — Crees, Cree people

nêhiyawêwin — Cree language

niciwâmiskwêw — "other me"; this term is used for the wife of an ex-husband; it is part of the complex cousin-terminology of Cree society *nikamona* — songs

nikâwiy — my mother

nikâwîs — an aunt from the female side (little mother or sub-mother)

nikotwâsik — the number "6"

nipahtâkêwin — murder

nipahisowin — suicide

nipiy — water

nisis — my uncle (mother's brother), my father-in-law

nihâhkômâkanak — my relatives

"niya ôma ki-kôhkom" — "I am your grandmother"

"niya oma nêhiyaw" — "I am Cree"

nohkom — my grandmother

nohtâwiy — my father

o

ocisîs — belly button

ohcinêmowin — verbal law that addresses the use of language against creation

ohcinêwin — the breaking of a law against anything other than a human being *ohpikinâwasowin* — child-rearing or raising

okicitâwak — describes "faith keepers"

okihcitâwiskwêw — singular (one) clan mother/warrior woman/lawkeeper

okihcitâwiskwêwak — many clan mothers/warrior women/lawkeepers

okihcitâwiskwêwikamik — clan mother/warrior/lawkeeper woman lodge

okimâw — chief/leader

okimâwâhtik — sundance lodge pole

okimâwaskwaciy — Chief Bear Hill in the Cypress Hills area

omâcîw — hunter

omâcîw nikamona — hunter songs

onîkânîwak — headmen

oskâpêwis — the sacred "helpers" (male and female) who lead the way for
any *nêhiyaw* gathering, event, or ceremony

oskiciy — pipestem

ôtênaw — used to describe a contemporary town or city, but in the days
before European contact describes a circle of tipis that are sacred

ô

ôhtêkwêwak — those persons who are born with the female and male genital characteristics, or hermaphrodites, which can be translated to mean
two-spirited

ôtênaw — used to describe a contemporary town or city, but in the days before European contact it described a circle of tipis that are sacred

p

pâst — to "go beyond or over"

pâstâho — indicates a transgression, or stepping over

pâstâhowin — "transgression" (nominalization of the verb by the ending -*win*; hence, *pâstâhowin*) — the breaking of a law against another human being

pâstâhowina — a person's many laws that they've broken

pâstâhw — verb that indicates that one transgresses against another

pâstâmow — "someone brings misfortune on himself by speech" — verbal breaking of a law against another human being

pâstâmowin — verbal law that addresses the use of language against human beings; misfortune provoked specifically by speech

pêpîsis — baby (newborn infant)

pimâcihowin — livelihood

pimâtisiwin — life

pîsim — the sun

pîwaya — the seeds that float in the air during the fall

s

sâh-sêwêham — Saysewahum; He Makes It (the Earth) Vibrate

simâkanisak — protectors that surrounded the living area but in contemporary terms used to describe police

t

tawâw niwâhkômâkanak — Welcome, my relatives

w

wâhkôhtowin — human kinships, as well as all of creation

wâhkôhmtowin — human kinships through blood line

wâspison — mossbag

wiyasiwêwina — human laws

wiyinikêwina — an act similar to a type of weaving

wîcêhtowin — relationship, getting along with one another

wîcêw — to come alongside or to support

wîhkask — one braid of sweetgrass

wîhkaskwa — more than one braid of sweetgrass, or unbraided sweetgrass

wîsahkêcâhk — described as a "trickster," but is part spirit and part man

wîsakîhîw — acts of wasting animal meat or other products (Woods Cree spelling)

Notes

Notes to the Introduction

1 James (Sa'ke'j) Youngblood Henderson, Marjorie L. Benson, Isobel M. Findlay. *Aboriginal tenure in the constitution of Canada*. Scarborough, Ont.: Carswell, 2000 (acknowledgements page, no page number).

2 Alfred Taiaiake. http://www.ammsa.com/node/23047, "Who Are You Calling Canadian?"

3 William Ratfoot, Dakota Summit, PowerPoint presentation, March 2010.

4 Harold Johnson, *Two Families: Treaties and Government*. Saskatoon: Purich Publishing Ltd., 2007, p. 13.

5 *Ibid.*

6 *Ibid.*, p. 27.

7 James (Sa'ke'j) Youngblood Henderson. *Treaty Rights in the Constitution of Canada*. Toronto: Thomson Canada, 2007, p. 151.

8 Sylvia McAdam. *Cultural Teachings: First Nations Protocols and Methodologies*. Saskatoon: Saskatchewan Indian Cultural Centre, 2009, p. 11.

9 *Ibid.*, p. 11.

Notes to Chapter Two

1 Sylvia McAdam. 2009, *Cultural Teachings: First Nations Protocols and Methodologies*. Saskatoon: Saskatchewan Indian Cultural Centre, 2009, p. 3.

2 Harold Cardinal and Walter Hildebrandt. *Treaty Elders of Saskatchewan: Our Dream is that Our Peoples Will One Day be Clearly Recognized as Nations*. Calgary: University of Calgary Press, 2000, p. 43.

3 Judie Bopp, PhD., Michael Bopp, PhD., and Phil Lane, Jr. *Aboriginal Domestic Violence in Canada*. Ottawa: Aboriginal Healing Foundation, 2006.

4 Neil Andersson and Amy Nahwegahbow. *Family Violence and the Need for Prevention Research in First Nations, Inuit, and Métis Communities*. http://www.ncbi.nlm.nih.gov/pmc/articles/PMC2962655/. Retrieved May 13, 2012.

5   Interview with Juliette McAdam (Saysewahum).

6   SaskPrevention, *Traditional Teachings*. Barry Ahenakew speaks in this video about *manitow iskotêw*. http://www.skprevention.ca/instructional-videos/#Sexual%20and%20Reproductive%20Health.

7   *Ibid.*

8   Twigg and Hengen. Going Back to the Roots: Using the Medicine Wheel in the Healing Process. *First Peoples Child and Family Review*, 2009.

9   Roberts, Harper, Tuttle-Eagle Bull and Heideman-Provost. The Native American Medicine Wheel and Individual Psychology: Common themes. *The Journal of Individual Psychology*, Vol. 5(1), 1998.

10 SaskPrevention, *Traditional Teachings*.

11 Interview with Juliette McAdam (Saysewahum) on the Whitefish Lake Reserve #118 on Nov. 6, 2010.

12 David G. Mandelbaum. *The Plains Cree*. Regina: Canadian Plains Research Centre, 1979, p. 230.

13 Interview with Juliette McAdam (Saysewahum).

14 David G. Mandelbaum. *The Plains Cree*, p. 225.

15 *Ibid.*, p. 225.

16 *Ibid.*, p. 328.

17 Freda Ahenakew and H. C. Wolfart (translators and editors). *Our Grandmothers' Lives, As Told in Their Own Words. Kohkominawak Otacimowiniwawa*. Saskatoon: Fifth House, 1992, p. 77.

18 Joseph F. Dion. *My Tribe the Crees*. Calgary: Glenbow Museum, 1979, p. 6.

19 *Ibid.*

20 Pamela D. Palmater. *Beyond Blood: Rethinking Indigenous Identity*. Saskatoon: Purich Publishing Ltd., p. 29.

21 http://www.ammsa.com/publications/windspeaker/who-you-calling-canadian-0.

Notes to Chapter Three

1   *wîsahkêcâhk* is believed to be part human and part spirit, big brother to humans and to creation. He has been referred to as a "trickster," a spiritual keeper, and is gifted with powers to heal and answer prayers.

2   Interview with Francis McAdam Saysewahum, Saskatoon, Oct. 11, 2014.

3   Robert Brightman. *Traditional Narratives of the Rock Cree Indians*. Gatineau, Que: Canadian Museum of History, 1980. p. 76.

4   John Borrows. *Creating Canada: Constructing an Indigenous Country.* Whelen Visiting Lectureship. Saskatoon: University of Saskatchewan Printing Services, 2005, p. 5.

5   *Ibid.*, p. 19.

6   Harold Johnson. *Two Families: Treaties and Government*. Saskatoon: Purich Publishing Ltd., 2007, p. 20.

7   Interview with Juliette McAdam (Saysewahum) at the Big River Reserve.

8   Sylvia McAdam. *Cultural Teachings: First Nations Protocols and Methodologies*. Saskatoon: Saskatchewan Indian Cultural Centre, 2009.

9   Interview with Francis McAdam Saysewahum at the Big River Reserve, Nov. 3, 2008.

10 Harold Johnson. *Two Families*, p. 13.

11 *Ibid.*

12 *Ibid.*, p. 27.

13 James (Sa'ke'j) Youngblood Henderson. *Treaty Rights in the Constitution of Canada*. Toronto: Thomson Canada Limited, 2007, p. 151.

14 Clay McLeod. "The Oral Histories of Canada's Northern People, Anglo-Canadian evidence law, and Canada's fiduciary duty to first nations: breaking down the barriers of the past." *Alberta Law Review*, Vol. 30, pp. 1276-1290.

15 *Ibid.*

16 David G. Mandelbaum. *The Plains Cree, An Ethnographic, Historical and Comparative Study*. Regina: Canadian Plains Research Center, 1979, p. 228.

17 Harold Cardinal and Walter Hildebrandt. *Treaty Elders of Saskatchewan: Our Dream is that Our Peoples Will One Day be Clearly Recognized As Nations.* Calgary: University of Calgary Press, 2000, p. 2.

18 Sylvia McAdam. *Cultural teachings*, p. 12.

19 David G. Mandelbaum. *The Plains Cree*, p. 228.

20 *Ibid.*, p. 229.

21 Interview with Francis McAdam (Saysewahum). This is a modern gift since the arrival of the Europeans. Money has replaced buffalo hides, moose hides, etc.

22 Harold Cardinal and Walter Hildebrandt. *Treaty Elders of Saskatchewan*, p. 2.

23 Interview with Francis McAdam Saysewahum at the Big River Reserve, Nov. 3, 2008.

24 Sylvia McAdam. *Cultural Teachings*, p. 8.

25 John Borrows. *Canada's Indigenous Constitution.* Toronto: University of Toronto Press, 2010, p. 85.

26 *Ibid.*

27 Harold Cardinal and Walter Hildebrandt. *Treaty Elders of Saskatchewan*, p. 7.

28 Interview with Juliette McAdam Saysewahum at the Big River Reserve, Nov. 3, 2008.

29 *Ibid.*

30 Office of the Treaty Commissioner. *Treaty Implementation: Fulfilling the Covenant.* Saskatoon: 2007, p. 93.

31 Robert Brightman. *Grateful Prey: Rock Cree Human-Animal Relationships.* Berkeley: University of California Press, 1993, p. 109.

32 *Ibid.*, p. 113.

33 *Ibid.*, p. 114.

34 *Ibid.*, p. 109.

35 *Ibid.*

36 *Ibid.*

37 Sylvia McAdam. *Cultural Teachings*, p. 8.

38 John Borrows. *Canada's Indigenous Constitution*, p. 85.

39 *Ibid.*, p. 85.

40 Robert Brightman. *Grateful Prey*, p. 110.

41 *Ibid.*, p. 110.

42 *Ibid.*, p. 117.

43 *Ibid.*

44 *Ibid.*

45 Alexander Morris, *The Treaties of Canada with the Indians of Manitoba and the North-West Territories*. Saskatoon: Fifth House, 1991, pp. 169 & 218.

46 *Ibid.*

47 *Ibid.*, p. 113.

48 *Ibid.*

49 Interview with Juliette McAdam Saysewahum at the Big River Reserve, Nov. 3, 2008.

50 *Ibid.*

51 Interview with Francis McAdam Saysewahum at the Big River Reserve, Nov. 3, 2008.

52 Harold Cardinal and Walter Hildebrandt. *Treaty Elders of Saskatchewan*, p. 3.

53 *Ibid.*

54 *Ibid.*, p. 8

55 Francis McAdam Saysewahum personal interview, Nov. 24, 2011.

56 Harold Cardinal and Walter Hildebrandt. *Treaty Elders of Saskatchewan*, p. 14.

57 *Ibid.*, p. 14.

58 Office of the Treaty Commissioner. *Treaty Implementation*, p. 93.

59 *Ibid.*

60 John Borrows, *Creating Canada*, p. 4.

61 Joseph F. Dion. *My Tribe the Crees*. Calgary: Glenbow Alberta Institute, 1979,

p. 7.

62 Sylvia McAdam. *Cultural Teachings*, p. 6.

63 Sylvia McAdam. *Cultural Teachings*, p. 30.

64 Eleanor Burke Leacock. *Myths of Male Dominance: Collected Articles on Women Cross-Culturally*. Chicago: Haymarket Books, 2008, p. 34.

65 *Ibid.*, p. 34.

66 Devon A. Mihesuah. *Natives and Academics: Researching and Writing about American Indians*. Lincoln: University of Nebraska Press, 1998. Quoted in Aaron B. Tootoosis, *Indigenous Studies 491* — First Nations University of Canada, Dr. Alexander Blair Stonechild, p. 2 (thesis paper).

67 Olive Patricia Dickason and William Newbigging. *A Concise History of Canada's First Nations*. Toronto: Oxford University Press, 2010, p. 16.

68 *Ibid.*, p. 31.

69 Interview with Francis McAdam (Saysewahum) on Aug. 15, 2009 on the Big River Reserve #118 (now referred to as Big River First Nation).

70 Francis McAdam (Saysewahum): *pîwaya* are the seeds that float in the fall and cover the air with puffs of white.

71 Sylvia McAdam. *Cultural Teachings*, p. 8.

72 Robert Brightman. *Grateful Prey*, p. 319.

73 James (Sa'ke'j) Youngblood Henderson. *Treaty Rights in the Constitution of Canada*. Toronto: Carswell, 2007, p. 317.

74 Interview with Francis McAdam (Saysewahum) on Aug. 15, 2009.

75 Robert Brightman, *Grateful Prey*, p. 281.

76 *Ibid.*, p. 283.

77 James (Sa'ke'j) Youngblood Henderson. *Treaty Rights in the Constitution of Canada*, p. 319.

78 *Ibid.*

79 Robert Brightman. *Grateful Prey*, p. 104.

80 *Ibid.*

81 *Ibid.*, p. 105

82 *Ibid.*

83 *Ibid.*, p. 106

84 Interview with Francis McAdam (Saysewahum) on Aug. 15th 2009.

85 *Ibid.*

86 Katherine Pettipas. *Severing the Ties that Bind.* Winnipeg: University of Manitoba Press, 1994, p. 46.

87 Diane Knight. *The Seven Fires: Teachings of the Bear Clan as Recounted by Dr. Dan Musqua.* Many Worlds Publishing, 2001, p. 36.

88 Sylvia McAdam. *Cultural Teachings*, p. 42.

89 This is my own translation from speaking with elders.

90 Royal Commission on Aboriginal Peoples, Vol. 3, Family, p. 12. http://caid.ca/RRCAP3.0.pdf.

91 Interview with Juliette McAdam (Saysewahum) on Aug. 15, 2009.

92 David G. Mandelbaum. *The Plains Cree*, p. 162.

93 *Ibid.*, p. 212.

94 Eleanor Burke Leacock. *Myths of Male Dominance*, retrieved May 14 2012: http://www.youtube.com/watch?v=1WPPO-M0t8w&feature=share.

95 Royal Commission on Aboriginal Peoples, Vol. 4, Perspectives and Realities; Chap. 2 — Women's Perspectives. http://www.collectionscanada.gc.ca/webarchives/20071211052616/http://www.ainc-inac.gc.ca/ch/rcap/sg/sj2_e.html.

96 William M. Graham. *Treaty Days: Reflections of an Indian Commissioner.* Calgary: Glenbow Museum, 1991, p. 17.

97 David G. Mandelbaum. *The Plains Cree*, p. 194.

98 Eleanor Burke Leacock. *Myths of Male Dominance.*

99 Interview with Juliette McAdam (Saysewahum) May 5th 2010, Big River Reserve.

100 Royal Commission on Aboriginal Peoples, Vol. 4, Perspectives and Realities; Chap. 2 — Women's Perspectives.

101 Amnesty International. http://www.amnesty.ca/our-work/issues/indigenous-peoples/no-more-stolen-sisters.

102 Alma Kytwayhat, South Dakota Language Summit, PowerPoint presentation, March 2010.

103 James (Sa'ke'j) Youngblood Henderson. *Treaty Rights in the Constitution of Canada*, p. 255.

104 *Ibid.*, p. 298.

105 David G. Mandelbaum. *The Plains Cree*, p. 127.

106 *Ibid.*

107 *Ibid.*, p. 125

108 *Ibid.*

109 *Ibid.*, p. 126.

110 Royal Commission on Aboriginal Peoples, Vol. 3, Family, p. 11.

111 Shared with me by my father, Francis McAdam (Saysewahum).

112 Robert Brightman. *Grateful Prey*, pp. 106-107.

113 *Ibid.*, p. 106.

114 Interview with Juliette McAdam (Saysewahum) on Aug. 15, 2009.

115 *Ibid.*

116 Winona Stevenson. *Calling Badger and the Symbols of the Spirit Language: The Cree Origins of the Syllabic System.* artsandscience.usask.ca/cdprofile/download.php?fileid=127, p. 20.

117 *Ibid.*

118 *Ibid.*, p. 21.

119 Interview with Juliette McAdam (Saysewahum) on Aug. 15, 2009.

120 *Ibid.*

121 *Ibid.*

Notes to Chapter Four

1 Jack Funk. *Outside, the Women Cried: The Story of the Surrender by Chief Thunderchild's Band of Their Reserve Near Delmas, Saskatchewan, 1908.* Lincoln, NE: Iuniverse, 2007.

2 Harold Cardinal and Walter Hildebrant. *Treaty Elders of Saskatchewan.* Calgary: University of Calgary Press, 2000, p. 70.

3 *Ibid.*

4 Marlene Brant Castellano. "Elders Teachings in the Twenty-first Century: A Personal Reflection," in David Long and Olive Patricia Dickason. *Visions of the Heart.* Third Edition. Don Mills: Oxford University Press, 2011, p. 3.

5 Robert Brightman. *Grateful Prey: Rock Cree Human-Animal Relationships.* Berkeley: University of California Press, 1993, p. 2.

6 *Ibid.*, p. 282.

7 *Ibid.*, p. 281.

8 Olive Patricia Dickason and William Newbigging. *A Concise History of Canada's First Nations.* Don Mills: Oxford University Press, 2010, p. 9.

9 *Ibid.*, p. 9.

10 *Ibid.*

11 *Ibid.*

12 Olive Patricia Dickason and William Newbigging. *A Concise History of Canada's First Nations*, p. 10.

13 *Ibid.*, p.10.

14 *Ibid.*

15 Alexander Morris. *The Treaties of Canada with the Indians of Manitoba and the North-West Territories including the Negotiations in which they were based.* Saskatoon: Fifth House Publishers, 1991, p. 211.

16 *Ibid.*, p. 228.

17 *Ibid.*, p. 267.

18 James (Sa'ke'j) Youngblood Henderson. *Treaty Rights in the Constitution of Canada.* Toronto: Thomson Canada Limited, 2007, p. 402.

19 Alexander Morris. *The Treaties of Canada with the Indians of Manitoba and the North-West Territories*, p. 204-205.

20 Roger Duhamel, F.R.S.C. *Copy Of Treaty No. 6, Between Her Majesty The Queen And The Plain And Wood Cree Indians And Other Tribes Of Indians At Fort Carlton, Fort Pitt And Battle River With Adhesions*. Ottawa: Queen's Printer And Controller of Stationery, 1964, p. 3.

21 *Beattie v. Canada*, 2001 CanLII 22180 (FC), para. 8.

22 *Ibid.*, para. 10.

23 *Ibid.*, para. 11.

24 *Ibid.*, generally.

25 Alexander Morris. *The Treaties of Canada with the Indians of Manitoba and the North-West Territories*, p. 209.

26 *Ibid.*, p. 170

27 James (Sa'ke'j) Youngblood Henderson. *Treaty Rights in the Constitution of Canada*, p. 311.

28 *Ibid.*

29 Interview with Francis McAdam (Saysewahum).

30 Alexander Morris. *The Treaties of Canada with the Indians of Manitoba and the North-West Territories*, p. 186.

31 James (Sa'ke'j) Youngblood Henderson. *Treaty Rights in the Constitution of Canada*, p. 424

32 *Ibid.*, p. 423.

33 Eric Tang. *Agriculture; The Relationship Between Aboriginal Farmers and Non-Aboriginal Farmers*. Saskatoon: The Western Development Museum and the Saskatchewan Indian Cultural Centre, 2003, at p. 4.

34 Sarah Carter. *Lost Harvests*. Montreal/Kingston: McGill-Queens University Press, 1990, p. 20.

35 http://www.aadnc-aandc.gc.ca/eng/1100100030285/1100100030289. Retrieved Oct. 14, 2014.

36 *Ibid.*

37 http://www.muskeglake.com/business/. Retrieved Oct. 15, 2014.

38 *Ibid.*

39 *Ibid.*

40 http://www.globalautonomy.ca/global1/glossary_pop.jsp?id=CO.0068. Retrieved Oct. 15, 2014.

41 http://scc-csc.lexum.com/scc-csc/scc-csc/en/item/14246/index.do.

42 *Ibid.*

43 *Ibid.*

44 Idle no More website, retrieved Dec. 22, 2014. http://www.idlenomore.ca/turn_the_tables#_ftn5.

45 *Ibid.*

46 http://www.afn.ca/uploads/files/sc/spec_-_report_on_joint_first_nations_-_canada_task_force_on_specific_claims_policy_reform.pdf. Retrieved Oct. 15, 2014.

47 http://www.globalautonomy.ca/global1/glossary_pop.jsp?id=CO.0068. Retrieved Oct. 15, 2014.

48 http://www.globalautonomy.ca/global1/glossary_pop.jsp?id=CO.0068. Retrieved Oct. 15, 2014 (cited from Archibald and Crnkovich, 1999; Archibald, Linda and Crnkovich, Mary, 1999). If gender mattered: A case study of Inuit women, land claims and the Voisey's Bay Nickel Project. Ottawa: Status of Women Canada. Available at http://www.swc-cfc.gc.ca./.

49 https://intercontinentalcry.org/scc-tsilhqotin-decision-canadas-first-nations-termination-policies/. Retrieved Oct. 15, 2014.

Notes to Chapter Five

1 http://www.ammsa.com/node/23047. "Who Are You Calling a Canadian?" p. 2.

2 Interview with Erland Terrance Atimoyoo, June 23, 2012, Saskatoon, Sask.

3 Olive Patricia Dickason and William Newbigging. *A Concise History of Canada's First Nations.* Oxford University Press Canada, 2010, p. 196.

4   James (Sa'ke'j) Youngblood Henderson. *Treaty Rights in the Constitution of Canada*. Toronto: Thomson Canada Limited, 2007, p. 272.

5   Alexander Morris. *The Treaties of Canada with the Indians of Manitoba and the North-West Territories including the Negotiations in which they were based*. Saskatoon: Fifth House Publishers, 1991, p. 168.

6   *Ibid.*

7   Sylvia McAdam. *Cultural Teachings: First Nations Protocols and Methodologies*. Saskatoon: Saskatchewan Indian Cultural Centre, 2009.

8   *The Historical Development of the Indian Act*. Treaties and Historical Research Centre, P.R.E. Group, Indian and Northern Affairs, August 1978. http://www.kitselas.com/images/uploads/docs/The_Historical_Development_of_the_Indian_Act_Aug_1978.pdf.

9   *Ibid.*, p. 1

10 *Ibid.*, p. 2.

11 *Ibid.*

12 *Ibid.*, p. 3

13 *Ibid.*, p. 11.

14 Katherine Pettipas. *Severing the Ties that Bind*. Winnipeg: University of Manitoba Press, 1994), p. 36.

15 John D. Whyte (Ed.), *Moving Toward Justice: Legal Traditions and Aboriginal Justice*. Saskatoon: Purich Publishing Ltd., in association with the Saskatchewan Institute of Public Policy, University of Regina, 2008, p. 54.

16 *Ibid.*, p. 54.

17 Katherine Pettipas. *Severing the Ties that Bind*, p. 65.

18. *Ibid.*, p. 65

19 Robert J. Castel and David Westfall, *Castel's English-Cree Dictionary and Memoirs of the Elders*. Brandon, Man.: Brandon University Northern Teacher Education Program, 2001, p. 525.

20 William M. Graham. *Treaty Days: Reflections of an Indian Commissioner*. Calgary: Glenbow Museum, 1991, p. 55.

21 Pamela D. Palmater. *Beyond Blood: Rethinking Indigenous Identity*. Saskatoon: Purich Publishing Ltd., 2011, p. 47.

22 Eric Robinson and Henry Bird Quinney. *The Infested Blanket: Canada's Constitution-Genocide of Indian Nations*. Winnipeg: Queenston House Publishing, 1985, p. 6-7.

23 Judith F. Sayers, Kelly McDonald, Jo-Anne Fiske, Melonie Newell, Evelyn George, and Wendy Cornet. "First Nations Women, Governance and the Indian Act: A Collection of Policy Research Reports," retrieved from http://www.swc-cfc.gc.ca/index-eng.html, Nov. 2001, p. 15.

24 Ward Churchill. *A little Matter of Genocide: Holocaust and Denial in the Americas 1492 to the Present*. San Francisco, City Light Books, 1997, p. 401.

25 *Ibid.*, p. 418.

26 *Ibid.*, p. 423.

27 First Nations Child and Family Services: http://www.fncaringsociety.com/. Retrieved May 20, 2012.

28 Antoon A. Leenaars, Jack Anowak, Colleen Brown, Trish Hill-Keddie, and Lucien Taparti. *Genocide and Suicide Among Indigenous People: The North meets the South*. http://www2.brandonu.ca/library/cjns/19.2/cjnsv19no2_pg337-363.pdf p. 348. Retrieved May 19, 2012.

29 Aboriginal Healing Foundation Research Series. *Response, Responsibility, and Renewal*. Ottawa: Aboriginal Healing Foundation, 2009, p. 221.

30 *Ibid.*, p. 181.

31 *Ibid.*, p. 182.

32 *Ibid.*, p. 182.

33 *Ibid.*, p. 182.

34 Ibid., p. 265.

35 Interview with Juliette McAdam (Saysewahum), May 14, 2012, in Whitefish Lake Reserve #118.

Notes to Chapter Six

1   http://www.thestar.com/opinion/editorials/2012/10/19/omnibus_budget_
bill_c45_is_an_affront_to-_democracy.html. Retrieved Oct. 13, 2014.

2   *Ibid.*

3   http://www.kapuskasingtimes.com/2013/01/16/bill-c-45-whats-all-the-fuss.
Retrieved Oct. 13, 2014.

4   http://www.cbc.ca/news/politics/22-changes-in-the-budget-bill-fine-
print-1.1233481. Retrieved Oct. 13, 2014.

5   *Ibid.*

6   http://www.ihraam.org/indigenous-Canada/IndianAct.html. Retrieved Oct.
15, 2014.

7   *Ibid.*

8   Idle No More website, retrieved Dec 22, 2014. http://www.idlenomore.ca/
turn_the_tables#_ftn5.